finals·series d
HOME·GAME 01

02 NBA FINALS

finals·series d
HOME·GAME 02

02 NBA FINALS

# DYNASTY!!!

## THE OFFICIAL NBA FINALS 2002 RETROSPECTIVE

BY JOHN HAREAS

PHOTOGRAPHY BY NBA ENTERTAINMENT PHOTOS

# 2001-02

"There's a certain sense of confidence that is abiding. There's a certain feeling that prevails, that come hell or high water we know how to rally our collective energies together to play, and to defend this championship." +++ PHIL JACKSON +++

## CREDITS

**DESIGNED AND PRODUCED BY:**
NVU Editions, 363 W Erie, Unit 4W, Chicago IL 60610

**PUBLISHED BY:**
Vulcan Sports Media, DBA The Sporting News
10176 Corporate Square Drive, Suite 200, St. Louis Mo 63132

**PHOTOGRAPHY BY: NBA ENTERTAINMENT PHOTOS**

The NBA and individual NBA member team identifications reproduced in and
on this publication are trademarks, copyrighted designs and other forms of intellectual
property of NBA Properties, Inc. and the respective NBA member teams and
may not be used, in whole or part, without the written consent of NBA Properties, Inc.

**THE OFFICIAL
2002 NBA FINALS RETROSPECTIVE**
Copyright © 2002 by NBA Properties, Inc.

All rights reserved under International and Pan-American Copyright Conventions.
Published in the United Stated by The Sporting News.

Library of Congress Cataloging-in-Publication Data is available from the publisher.

ISBN 0-89204-694-5
Printed in the Unites States of America
9 8 7 6 5 3 2

[FIRST EDITION]

IN MEMORY OF STEVEN FRANK STROBERT: A HUSBAND AND FATHER,
A FRIEND AND NEIGHBOR AND ONE PASSIONATE SPORTS FAN.

November 10, 1967 - September 11, 2001

· · · · · · · · · · · · · · · · · · · · · · · · · · · · · · + + + · · · · · · · · · · · · · · · · · · · · · · · · · · · · · ·

## ACKNOWLEDGEMENTS

What a joyous basketball journey. Fresh off the 30 day, sleep deprived Where's Walton? Love It Live Tour and head first into a "crash" book documenting the Los Angeles Lakers historic championship run...*Some Folks Got Fortune... Some Got Eyes Of Blue...What You Got Will Always See You Through... You're A Lucky Man...*The Love It Live spirit and passion of its leader, Bill Walton, are forever instilled ...*Throw It Down, Big Man!, Throw It Down!*...However, with all due respect to Captain Jack, Ken Kesey and the Merry Pranksters, this NBA band of jovial men working on this project was beyond compare... Driving this *Retrospective* Bus was Charlie Rosenzweig, providing the direction and dreams for yours truly...*Big Wheels Roll Through Fields...Where Sunlight Streams...Meet Me In A Land Of Hope And Dreams*...Joe Amati and Michael Levine...*Dedication Baby Through And Through...Dedication Like I Give To You*...the lead Merry Pranksters, applying meticulous attention to detail regarding photos, copy and overall look and feel of this beautifully designed book... *Hail! to the victors valiant...Hail! to the conquering heroes*...Carmin Romanelli ...*I Am The Lizard King*...adding his creative touch throughout the process...

*Spirits in the night, all night*...Scott Yurdin, Dave Bonilla, John Kristofick and Bennett Renda handling the painstaking photo research and high-res    . process...*We Swore Forever Friends On The Backstreets Until The End*...Andy Bernstein, Nat Butler, Jesse Garrabrant and all of the great NBA Entertainment photographers...*Talk About A Dream, Try to Make It Real*...David Mintz, the point man for research and statistics along with the rest of the All-Star lineup, Mario Argote, Chris Countee and Luke Gorman.

*With That Long Night's Journey In Your Eyes*...Thanks to everyone at NVU Productions, particularly Jim Forni and Steve Polacek, the lead designer whose singular focus, commitment and terrific design talent along with Heather Crosby's made this project happen flawlessly...Steve Meyerhoff at The Sporting News...

*My Love Will Not Let You Down*...Lastly and most importantly: A *huge thank you* to Jennifer, Emma and Christopher whose love and support is boundless...*My Love Will Not Let You Down.*

John Hareas—June 2002

## SPECIAL THANKS

### AT NBA ENTERTAINMENT PHOTOS
Carmin Romanelli, Joe Amati, Jesse Garrabrant, David Bonilla, Pam Healy,  Michael Klein,
Scott Yurdin, Brian Choi, John Kristofick, Bennett Renda

### AT NBA ENTERTAINMENT
Adam Silver, Gregg Winik, Heidi Ueberroth, Charles Rosenzweig, Paul Hirschheimer,  Marc Hirschheimer,
Michael Levine, Mario Argote, David Mintz, Chris Countee, Luke Gorman, Meredith Tanchum

### AT THE NBA
David Stern, Russ Granik, Tim Andree, Brian McIntyre, Terry Lyons

### AT NVU PRODUCTIONS
Jim Forni, Steve Polacek, Melinda Fry, Tim Sheridan, Elizabeth Fulton, Sue Young

### AT THE SPORTING NEWS
Kathy Kinkeade, Steve Meyerhoff, Marilyn Kasal, David Walton, Anna Jones

### ALSO
Phil Jackson, Jeanie Buss, Mitch Kupchak, Jim Perzik, John Black, Tim Harris,
Keith Harris and the entire Lakers organization

Byron Scott, Rod Thorn, Lou Lamoriello, Chris Modrzynski, Leo Ehrline, Gary Sussman,
Aaron Harris and the entire Nets organization

## PHOTOGRAPHY CREDITS

| | | | |
|---|---|---|---|
| RAY AMATI | 87, 88, 89, 92 | ANDY HAYT | 25 |
| ANDREW D. BERNSTEIN | 1, 2–3, 6–7, 8, 10, 11, 14, 16, 19, 21, 24, 26, 28, 29, 30, 31, 32, 34, 35, 37, 38–39, 40–41, 42, 43, 44, 45, 46, 47, 49, 50, 51, 52, 53, 54–55, 57, 58 59, 60, 61, 62, 63, 64–65, 67,69, 71, 73, 74, 75, 76–77, 80, 81, 83, 89, 90, 91, 93, 95, 96, 98, 99, 100, 101, 103, 104, 108, 109, 112, (FRONT AND BACK COVER) | HARRY HOW╱GETTY IMAGES | 61 |
| | | JED JACOBSOHN╱GETTY IMAGES | 106 |
| | | M.DAVID LEEDS | 86, 87, 89 |
| | | MARK MAINZ╱GETTY IMAGES | 88, 89 |
| DAVID BLANK | 74, 80, 86 | ROBERT MORA | 23, 48 |
| MATT BROWN | 88 | SCOTT QUINTARD | 15, 16, 86, 87, 88, 89 |
| VINCE BUCCI╱GETTY IMAGES | 86,87,88,89 | DICK RAPHAEL | 23 |
| NATHANIEL S. BUTLER | 27, 44, 66, 70, 72, 78, 79, 82, 83, 85, 94, 107, 109 | BILL SMITH | 20 |
| GARRETT W. ELLWOOD | 18 | CATHERINE STEENKESTE | 12, 13 |
| SAM FORENCICH | 46, 52, 56, 57 | NOREN TROTMAN | 83, 97, 102, 104, 105 |
| JESSE D. GARRABRANT | 68, 104, 110–111 | ROCKY WIDNER | 36, 45, 46, 61, 62, 84 |
| BARRY GOSSAGE | 46 | | |
| NOAH GRAHAM | 16, 17, 33, 51 | | |

# CONTENTS

# THE LONGEST SEASON

+++ BY PHIL JACKSON +++

The 'team' had dined at five tables in a meeting room at the Hilton Hotel in Honolulu, HI. We had arrived that afternoon on a flight from L.A. to begin our training at the U of Hawaii. I looked at 19 faces, over half of them new players to me. It wasn't the way I'd envisioned beginning the defense of a championship, let alone attempt the back-to-back-to-back feat.

Shaq had an operation on his toe in September; he would be sidelined for a couple more weeks. Mark Madsen and Derek Fisher had gone through surgery in July and would need most of the month to recuperate. Kobe's grandfather had died two days before camp and he was with his family in Philly for the rest of the week. Horace Grant, Ron Harper and Ty Lue were all gone from the team. Hmm, where do I even start?

*This year you will find a greater challenge than last year, and some of you know how difficult it was for us last year. You will be playing games to which each team will bring their "A" game, and their fans will anticipate for weeks in advance to see how their home boys match-up. You will see the best of the NBA and sometimes feel like you're playing at your worst—even the officials will challenge you nightly to make sure you know that you won't be allowed to coast or get away without showing your championship spirit and will.*

*It has always been the most difficult season from my experience. Winning during the season and in the playoffs will have a special feeling for you this year. You know my adage about championships*

*not being won in October or November. Yet, know that the habits you form and the professionalism you bring to work day in and day out lends itself to color the season from the first day you step on the court till the last. Tomorrow is to be our first practice day. Make sure you not only heed my words, but also understand them.*

*Now, on a personal note, I might not be here to help you toe the line. My mother is going through a very rough time and she might not live through the week, and like Kobe, I may need to be back with my family. The coaching staff can handle my absence—their word is my word—besides, Tex will look forward to holding your feet to the fire.*

It was two days later that my brother called at 8 a.m. and told me my mother had died early in the morning on October 5th. I booked a flight and left that day for Montana. I had no qualms about leaving the training of this team to my staff. I needed to be with my immediate family. I missed the next week of camp and beat the team back to L.A. In the process they lost the first two exhibition games in Honolulu and were ready to get back to our base in El Segundo.

Shaq began to practice the next week and we got back to work in earnest. In fact, we began the season in great form, going 16-1 to get out of the blocks, and at that time people were declaring us the champs and chiding the rest of the NBA about its ability to compete. My players were even talking about maybe challenging winning 70 games.

Meanwhile, Dallas and Sacramento were almost keeping stride with us and we had just passed the easiest part of our schedule. But, it wasn't until after a game in Houston, when Shaq played under restriction in Memphis that we really came to grips with the fact that we were going to have to punch our way through the season. Shaq made the first of two visits to the injured reserve list where he spent the minimum of five games rehabilitating his toe and foot due to an arthritic big toe. The injury and limitation put on Shaquille was to color our season. The injury limited the movement of Shaq's foot, because every extreme action of jumping or stopping put pressure on a joint that had become inflamed. I think playing every other game over an 82 game season just wore on his ability to play in pain night in and night out. We were going to have to find a way to win with him playing at 75 percent at best.

Kobe had to carry the pennant for the Lakers 2001-2002 season. He grew into the role of leader and carried us through some difficult stretches during the season. In October, I wanted to name another captain to accompany Shaq. I asked Kobe if he felt he was ready to become a co-captain and accept a role that Ron Harper had provided for the team the past two years. I asked him to sit on his decision for a day and come back to me with his answer, and that I was going to name Rick Fox as a co-captain regardless. The next day Kobe told me he felt he was ready and able to be a captain, even at age 23. I had talked to Kobe about this time in his career some two years earlier when I had inherited this Laker team. Kobe hadn't shown the ability to move from player to player and accept them as professionals, regardless of their ages, strengths or weaknesses. He wanted to lead by action solely, not with persuasion and psychology to encourage and motivate. I was pleased and proud of him when I'd learned that he had taken time out during the off-season to call his

teammates and talk to them about staying in shape and getting ready to win another one. He had become a leader.

The season ended without the nine-game winning streak we had run off the season before. We had little momentum leading into the playoffs with Portland. Maybe the only motivating force was a loss we'd suffered in Portland the last Sunday of the season, when the T-Blazers had come from behind to tie, then win a dramatic game in two overtimes.

They had celebrated the victory in an overstated fashion by jumping on the scorer's table and playing up to their home crowd. Yes, there was the Kobe Bryant-Ruben Patterson contest that waged Ruben's claim to be a "Kobe stopper."

The first round would be as dramatic as all three of our playoffs against the Western Conference opponents. We had won both home games at the Staples Center, but knew that Portland was a lot tougher on their home court. They made the usual charge during the fourth quarter by going to their

small, quick lineup, moving Wallace to center and making Shaq guard a three-point shooting big man and playing four quick, aggressive players on other players. They had scored to go up by eight points with thirty-some seconds to go in the game, when I called a time-out. We went to our score-press-foul mode of play when things get desperate. We scored via a Rick Fox quick basket. They missed a foul shot. Lakers scored on a three-point shot via Kobe. Portland makes one of two foul shots, etc., until Rob Horry buried a three-point shot with two seconds to go in front of the Blazer bench leaving them without hope. It was dramatic...Lakers win in three games.

Our next opponent, San Antonio, has become a great rival the past four seasons. The year before I came to L.A., they had won the title in the lockout-shortened season by beating the Lakers in a four-game sweep. The next year was shortened for them, as Tim Duncan had been injured during the playoffs, but they had been the best team in the league in 2000-2001, and we had swept them during the playoffs to set up a great series.

We played through the first game, which was bothering, as both Shaq and Kobe missed time on the floor due to injuries that required medical attention—a fortunate victory. The next game, San Antonio came out and played an aggressive solid game and held a lead in the second quarter of 17 points. We had fought back to get a chance to win at the end, but Kobe missed a contested lay-up and we couldn't hit a three-pointer to pull off the comeback.

After that game, I spent some time with our regulars in a video session looking at video tape. I was concerned about the activity of our defense and particularly our rebounding. Shaq had collected 7 rebounds in 41 minutes, a low number for a player of his capabilities.

During a run by San Antonio in the second quarter, I stopped the tape at one particular low point and asked Shaq if he was tired at this juncture of the game.

He said no. I said he looked like it because he wasn't pursuing the ball on rebounds.

I said, if need be, I'd play him 32 minutes a game rather than 40 if it meant his being more active on the boards and at the defensive end of the court. Shaq, although he wasn't happy about my critique, accepted his role as our leader on defense. He seemed to play right through his injured toe and we got back on the right track. It was at this point that our playoff season and temperament took on a new direction.

The San Antonio series was really dramatic in its own right. We had games right down to the wire in San Antonio and managed to win both coming back in the fourth quarter.

It seemed that no matter what Tim Duncan, the MVP, did, he couldn't find the right time to lift his team to victory. One of the most spectacular plays in the playoffs came in Game 3 in San Antonio. At the end of the game, Kobe had the ball with an opportunity to score, and lost the ball. The loose ball was recovered by Derek Fisher, who forced a tough shot with the clock running down. The rebound went high in the air and Kobe, on the run, grabbed the ball from three seven footers and put in a tough shot to give us the lead and the victory. We had won the pivotal game.

After the Spurs series, we met our in-state rival Sacramento Kings. They had a great year, winning 61 games and winning home court advantage during the playoffs. The series was piqued by the back-talk of the players. One of the leaders of the Kings, Vlade Divac, had claimed that if we didn't have the home court advantage they would win our series. They almost did.

It was a seesaw series. We won one on their home court and then they won the next on their own court. It was in that second game that Kobe Bryant had food poisoning, and after a rough night and some IV's, he managed to still play, although he was far from fit. They won Game 3 at Staples, and suddenly we had our backs to the wall for Game 4. This was the game that they pulled out to a 40-10 lead in the first quarter. We had to fight our way back from 27 points behind to finally win it on the last shot of the game by Robert Horry. It was another dramatic victory and one that left the Kings puzzled.

We had fought our way back to within two points with seven seconds left in the game. Kobe had gone to the basket on a drive and missed a contested shot, Shaq had a rebound attempt, and then a slapped ball headed towards Rob at the top of the key. He picked up the ball, loaded up his shot, and let it go. It was a shot that seemed to take forever. The buzzer went off, the fans stood-up to watch, and finally it swished—a three-pointer for the victory. It was one of those games that no one will forget, if they saw the effort of the teams and the drama of the last quarter.

Game 5 was a tight game, but we seemingly had it in hand. Shaq had fouled out of the game with over three minutes left, after being in foul trouble almost the entire game. We had managed to barely hold on to the lead when, on a desperate end-game possession, there was a loose ball. Rob Horry and Chris Webber both lunged towards it. The ball seemingly was tapped by Webber and went out of bounds and Webber despaired while still on the floor. But not to be. Ref Jack Nies called it Kings' ball. On the subsequent play Mike Bibby cashed in on an 18-foot jumper to give the Kings a one-point lead and the victory. Kings up in the series 3-2. It was a game I called "tit-for-tat."

Game 6 and Game 7 were closely contested games, which the Lakers won to bring the championship along with it. The seventh game especially should be mentioned because after Game 6, in which Shaq and Kobe had scored over 70 of our 100 points, the whole team had to contribute to gain the victory. It should also be mentioned that it was an overtime game that

carried great drama, and that the Kings can look back at it and feel gratified by their effort, even though a lot was made of the fact they missed almost half of their free throws.

The reason the Lakers won can be put down to be the greatness of their two stars. Shaq and Kobe were great when the Lakers needed them to play big games to win. However, in that last game, the team effort showed what poise and confidence this group had in each other. They showed the character of a champion; win or lose. After the game I had many people come to me and ask about their ability to focus and keep the pressure of the game from affecting their play. The word had spread that they had used meditation in the morning before that afternoon game.

That, of course, was my answer, but don't read too much into that, we do this before most games. They first sat in silence with the desire to do this together. "Let's do the right thing needed to be successful." Then they were able to go out and make reality of their desire. They weren't afraid of the outcome, because they knew they had put their whole-hearted effort into the game. It was the ability to play without pressure that led to good decisions and effective play. Oh, yes, lest I forget, Robert Horry hit another dramatic three-point shot in the last minutes of Game 7.

The NBA Finals were a bit anticlimactic, because the drama of the finals of the West had overshadowed them. The Nets had a wonderful season, but they didn't have the experience to deal with Shaquille O'Neal and the three-time champion Los Angeles Lakers.

Shaq seemed to get more effective each game during the playoffs, and by the last game of the Finals, he was playing extremely efficiently, passing, scoring, rebounding and blocking shots. He was named MVP for the Finals for the third year in a row. Yes, Rob Horry hit a big three down the stretch in the finals, Kobe was spectacular himself and the rest of the Lakers played up to their game, but it was Shaquille's final.

We realize the good fortune of winning three consecutive years. It takes good energy, good character, and good luck to win the title three times. So many things can defeat a good team, from internal discord to external injuries. I'm very proud of this team and we don't feel we've reached our limits yet. The drive is internal in this team to win again and to have dynasty associated with their name. As I work and watch this group accomplish their goals, I wish them well.

"Go on you Lakes."

**T**hey gathered as early as 3 a.m., dotting the Staples Center parking lot in purple and gold, a full 10 hours before their heroes would triumphantly arrive to greet the thousands upon thousands of well wishers. As dawn approached, Figueroa Boulevard featured patches of No. 8 and 34 jerseys, along with the likes of Horry and Fisher, while other fans chose to pay homage to Lakers legends West, Abdul-Jabbar and Johnson. Homemade signs soon lined the Boulevard—*Bling Dynasty*—*Shaquille Is Our*

*Superman*—*Thanks, Horry!!*—while purple and yellow foam fingers were out in full force.

The Los Angeles Lakers' championship parade had yet to begin, but judging by the fans' anticipation and enthusiasm, this annual rite of passage here in Southern California has hardly grown old. This is the third year in a row Lakers fans have flocked to the streets of downtown Los Angeles to pay tribute to basketball greatness, and each year the champions are celebrated with

even more passion and vigor than the ones before.

A mere 36 hours had passed since the Lakers accomplished a convincing sweep of the New Jersey Nets in the NBA Finals, giving them the honor of becoming only the fifth team in NBA history to win three consecutive titles. No more talk of being "close to a dynasty," because they have now earned that lofty distinction. Just ask the thousands of fans. Shaquille O'Neal's domination of the Nets in the

# CHAMPIONS

LOS ANGELES LAKERS
STAPLES
STAPLES Center
STAPLES Center
LOS ANGELES LAKERS
NBA 2002 CHAMPIONS
MPLS
8

series—36.3 points, 12.3 rebounds—earned him MVP honors, placing him in exclusive company. He and Michael Jordan are the only players to win three consecutive NBA Finals MVP awards. An achievement that certifies his status as one of the greatest big men to ever play the game.

At approximately 10:45 a.m., the Lakers' double-decker team buses pulled up to City Hall, where 3,000 fans had gathered, anxiously waiting to get the party started. Los Angeles

Mayor James K. Hahn greeted the crowd and awarded O'Neal and Bryant proclamations, declaring Friday Lakers Day in Los Angeles. The Governor of California, Gray Davis, followed suit, bestowing the same honor on behalf of the state. The Laker Girls took the stage under a blizzard of confetti, working the crowd into a frenzy, as Randy Newman's classic, "I Love L.A.," blared over the loudspeakers. The team thanked the fans and triumphantly hoisted all three

championship trophies, which glistened on this perfectly clear and sunny California day. It was now time for the team to re-enter the buses for the two-mile journey south down Figueroa to the Staples Center.

Chants of MVP! MVP!! MVP!!! greeted Shaquille O'Neal as he held up three fingers to the adoring crowd while Kobe Bryant and Robert Horry were basking in the chants praising their clutch playoff performances. Fans, who crowded

the sidewalks six and seven people deep, were deliriously waving brooms and blowing on purple and gold horns. Others were feverishly snapping pictures of their favorite players. A total of 11 double-decker buses carrying players and family members, along with two firetrucks featuring the Laker Girls and the Laker Band, slowly made their way through downtown Los Angeles to the Staples Center parking lot.

. . . . . . . . . . . . . . . . . . . . . + + + . . . . . . . . . . . . . . . . . . . .

**AS THE BUSES AND TRUCKS PULLED UP TO THEIR FINAL DESTINATION SHORTLY BEFORE 1:00, AN ESTIMATED CROWD OF 150,000 FANS WEARING PURPLE AND GOLD EAGERLY AWAITED THEIR ARRIVAL.**

. . . . . . . . . . . . . . . . . . . . . + + + . . . . . . . . . . . . . . . . . . . .

Chick Hearn, the legendary Hall of Fame Lakers broadcaster who experienced a difficult year that saw him overcome open heart surgery and a broken hip, served as emcee and introduced the players who emerged one by one from under the stage.

"I told you we would win back-to-back-to-back," said a jubilant Kobe Bryant, wearing an old school Minneapolis Lakers jersey featuring his No. 8. "We have the greatest coach, the most

dominant center, and the best fans. See you back here next year!"

Bryant enjoyed another terrific postseason in L.A.'s historic march to dynasty status, averaging 26.6 points and solidifying his reputation as one of the game's premier clutch fourth-quarter players.

While chants of three-peat were heard throughout the crowd, it was apparent that the coaches and players weren't satisfied with their recent historic accomplishment and were already embracing the challenge of becoming the first team since the 1960s Boston Celtics to win four titles in a row.

"We're going for four!," said reserve Mark Madsen in Spanish and then led the crowd in a chant of "Quatro, Quatro, Quatro." Madsen then received encouragement from Hearn and the team to break out in his Mad Dog herky-jerky dance, which has now become an annual Lakers celebration tradition. The swelling crowd roared as Madsen strutted his quirky moves as a beaming O'Neal led chants of 'Go, Mad Dog!,' 'Go, Mad Dog.'

"I'm calling it a four-feat, not a four-peat, because it would be incredible to do it," said

coach Phil Jackson, who now has coached three different teams to three consecutive titles. It was a triumphant postseason for Jackson, who not only tied Red Auerbach for most championship titles with nine but also became the NBA's all-time leader in playoff victories with 156, surpassing Pat Riley.

"Red, when you see this, thanks a lot," said an appreciative Jackson to the crowd, acknowledging Auerbach for the congratulatory note the Hall of Famer sent.

Fittingly, the celebration came to a close when sounds from the theme song, Superman, filled the air as O'Neal grabbed the microphone and took control of the proceedings.

......................... + + + .........................

"WE'LL BE BACK NEXT YEAR," SAID O'NEAL. "WE WANT TO GET NO.10 FOR PHIL JACKSON, THE GREATEST COACH IN THE WORLD. PUT THEM FOURS UP! PUT THEM FOURS UP I SAID!"

......................... + + + .........................

O'Neal then stoked an already simmering rivalry between the Sacramento Kings and the Lakers, two teams that battled down to the

wire in the thrilling seven-game Western Conference Finals, when he said:

"This is what I want you to teach your children today. Sacramento will never be the capital of California. Los Angeles is the new capital of California."

The crowd erupted.

Championships begin in the offseason with hard work and dedication, so it came as little surprise when Bryant admitted immediately following the Lakers' Game 4 triumph against the Nets that he spoke to his teammates about the task ahead in defending what is theirs.

"I talked to all the guys and got everybody on the same page as far as working out," said Bryant. "Because, some guys have had two months, a month and a half off. They're plotting. They're waiting. I'm sure Sacramento's working out right now. And we're not going to let our guards down. We're going to come back next year ready to play. They're going to try to take what we have and we're going to be waiting for them."

A declaration the 28 remaining NBA teams can undoubtedly do without. + + +

**W**hat is the true definition of a dynasty? How does a team achieve such a lofty status? In the 56-year history of the NBA, only a select number of teams have sustained championship excellence over an extended period of time: Minneapolis Lakers (1950s) • Boston Celtics (1960s and '80s) • Los Angeles Lakers (1980s) • Chicago Bulls (1990s). Now, the 21st Century Los Angeles Lakers are members of this exclusive group. The Lakers' accomplishment has also placed them on the short list of most distinguished dynasties. Only the Minneapolis Lakers (1952-54), Boston Celtics (1959-66) and Chicago Bulls (1991-93; 1996-98) have won three or more titles in a row.

The Lakers' three-peat now invites comparisons to these other great dynasties, begging the question—how do they stack up? How would Bill Russell defend Shaquille O'Neal in a Celtics-Lakers match up? Would Shaq, Kobe Bryant and the Lakers defeat Michael Jordan, Scottie Pippen and the Chicago Bulls in a seven-game series? And how would Phil Jackson, the coach of the Lakers, plot his strategy against Phil Jackson, the coach of the Bulls? Comparing dynasties from different eras is a never-ending debate. Different sets of rules, expansion—there are a multitude of factors that are unique to each era. There are simply no clear-cut winners. But the possibilities are certainly intriguing. + + +

# DYNASTY DEBATE

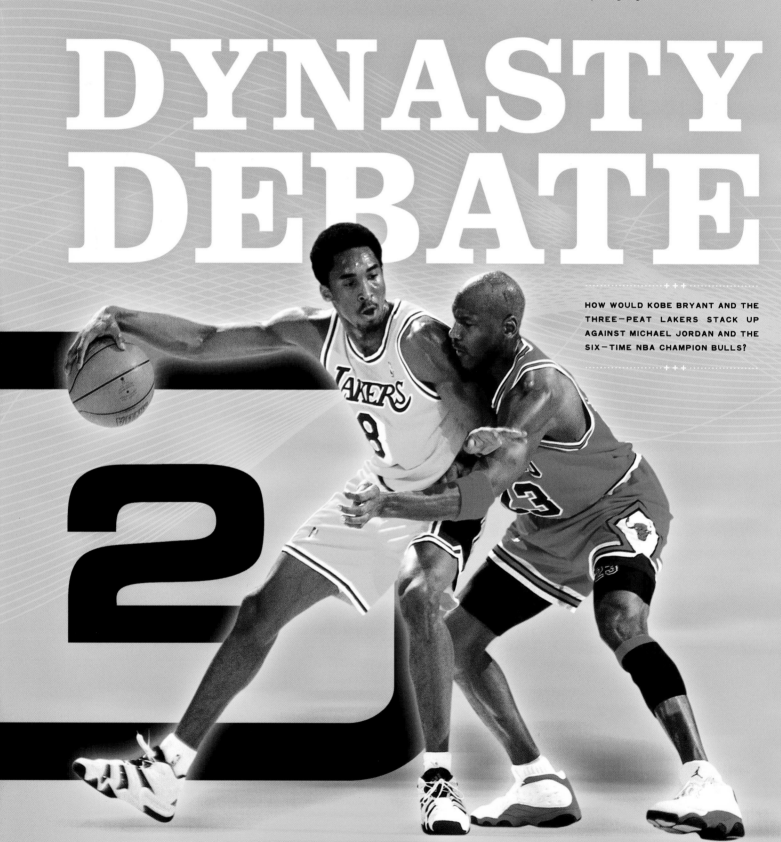

HOW WOULD KOBE BRYANT AND THE THREE—PEAT LAKERS STACK UP AGAINST MICHAEL JORDAN AND THE SIX—TIME NBA CHAMPION BULLS?

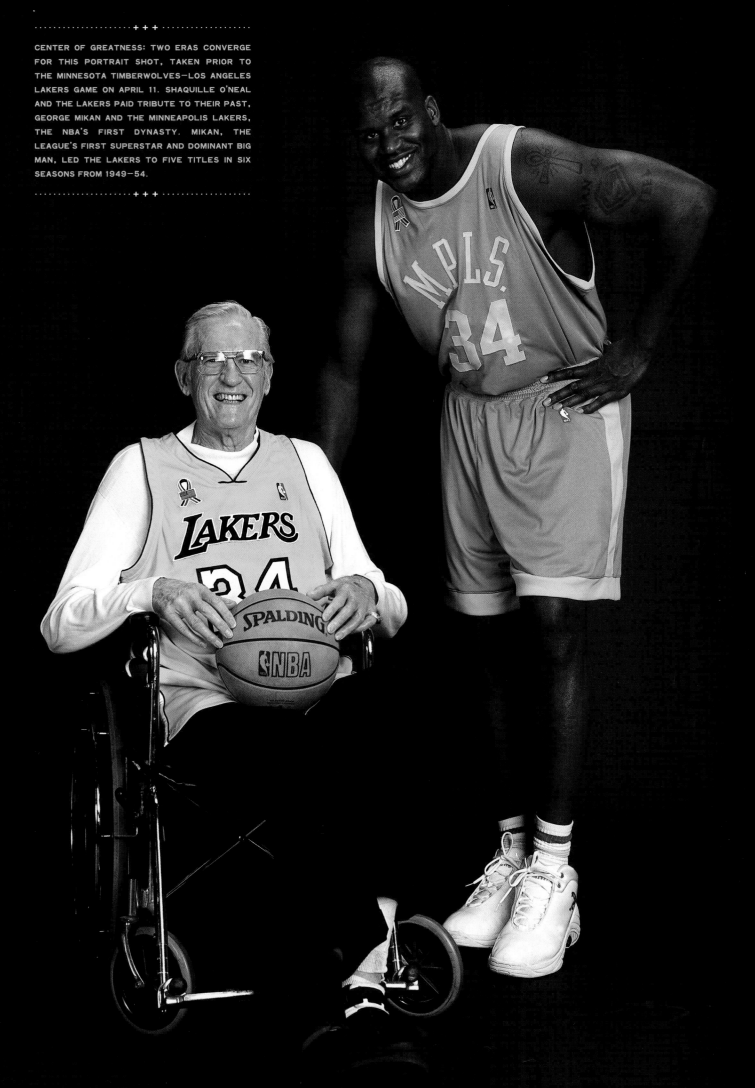

CENTER OF GREATNESS: TWO ERAS CONVERGE FOR THIS PORTRAIT SHOT, TAKEN PRIOR TO THE MINNESOTA TIMBERWOLVES—LOS ANGELES LAKERS GAME ON APRIL 11. SHAQUILLE O'NEAL AND THE LAKERS PAID TRIBUTE TO THEIR PAST, GEORGE MIKAN AND THE MINNEAPOLIS LAKERS, THE NBA'S FIRST DYNASTY. MIKAN, THE LEAGUE'S FIRST SUPERSTAR AND DOMINANT BIG MAN, LED THE LAKERS TO FIVE TITLES IN SIX SEASONS FROM 1949–54.

MINNEAPOLIS LAKERS 1951–1952      MINNEAPOLIS LAKERS 1952–1953      MINNEAPOLIS LAKERS 1953–1954

BOSTON CELTICS 1958–1959      BOSTON CELTICS 1959–1960      BOSTON CELTICS 1961–1962

CHICAGO BULLS 1990–1991      CHICAGO BULLS 1991–1992      CHICAGO BULLS 1992–1993

CHICAGO BULLS 1995–1996      CHICAGO BULLS 1996–1997      CHICAGO BULLS 1997–1998

# 1952-54
## MINNEAPOLIS LAKERS
Overall Reg. Season Record: 134 Wins 74 Losses (.644)
Overall Playoff Record: 27 Wins 11 Losses (.711)
Overall Playoffs Avg. Margin of Victory: 9.1 Points

# 1959-61
## BOSTON CELTICS
Overall Reg. Season Record: 168 Wins 58 Losses (.743)
Overall Playoff Record: 24 Wins 10 Losses (.706)
Overall Playoff Avg. Margin of Victory: 15.2 Points

# 1991-93
## CHICAGO BULLS
Overall Reg. Season Record: 185 Wins 61 Losses (.752)
Overall Playoff Record: 45 Wins 13 Losses (.776)
Overall Playoff Avg. Margin of Victory: 12.2 Points

---

### HEAD COACH: JOHN KUNDLA — 1951-52

Regular Season:
**40-26**
(.606)
Leading Scorer
George Mikan
(23.8)

Leading Rebounder
George Mikan
(13.5)

Assist Leader
Slater Martin
(3.8)

**PLAYOFF RESULTS:**
**Western Div. Semifinals:**
Minneapolis 2, Indianapolis 0
**Western Div. Finals:**
Minneapolis 3, Rochester 1
**NBA Finals:**
Minneapolis 4, New York 3

**Overall Playoff Record:**
9 Wins 4 Losses (.692)
**Playoffs Avg.**
**Margin of Victory:**
7.9 Points

### HEAD COACH: RED AUERBACH — 1958-59

Regular Season:
**52-20**
(.722)
Leading Scorer
Bill Sharman
(20.4)

Leading Rebounder
Bill Russell
(23.0)

Assist Leader
Bob Cousy
(8.6)

**PLAYOFF RESULTS:**
**Eastern Div. Finals:**
Boston 4, Syracuse 3
**NBA Finals:**
Boston 4, Minneapolis 0

**Overall Playoff Record:**
8 Wins 3 Losses (.727)
**Overall Playoff Avg.**
**Margin of Victory:**
13.0 Points

### HEAD COACH: PHIL JACKSON — 1990-91

Regular Season:
**61-21**
(.744)
Leading Scorer
Michael Jordan
(31.5)

Leading Rebounder
Horace Grant
(8.5)

Assist Leader
Scottie Pippen
(6.2)

**PLAYOFF RESULTS:**
**Eastern Conf. First Round:**
Chicago 3, New York 0
**Eastern Conf. Semifinals:**
Chicago 4, Philadelphia 1
**Eastern Conf. Finals:**
Chicago 4, Detroit 0
**NBA Finals:**
Chicago 4, L.A. Lakers 1

Overall Playoff Record:
15 Wins 2 Losses (.882)
**Overall Playoff Avg.**
**Margin of Victory:**
12.7 Points

---

### HEAD COACH: JOHN KUNDLA — 1952-53

Regular Season:
**48-22**
(.686)
Leading Scorer:
George Mikan
(20.6)

Leading Rebounder:
George Mikan
(14.4)

Assist Leader:
Slater Martin
(3.6)

**PLAYOFF RESULTS:**
**Western Div. Semifinals:**
Minneapolis 2, Indianapolis 0
**Western Div. Finals:**
Minneapolis 3, Fort Wayne 2
**NBA Finals:**
Minneapolis 4, New York 1

**Overall Playoff Record:**
9 Wins 3 Losses (.750)
**Playoffs Avg.**
**Margin of Victory:**
8.6 Points

### HEAD COACH: RED AUERBACH — 1959-60

Regular Season:
**59-16**
(.787)
Leading Scorer:
Tom Heinsohn
(21.7)

Leading Rebounder:
Bill Russell
(24.0)

Assist Leader:
Bob Cousy
(9.5)

**PLAYOFF RESULTS:**
**Eastern Div. Finals:**
Boston 4, Philadelphia 2
**NBA Finals:**
Boston 4, St. Louis 3

**Overall Playoff Record:**
8 Wins 5 Losses (.615)
**Overall Playoff Avg.**
Margin of Victory:
15.5 Points

### HEAD COACH: PHIL JACKSON — 1991-92

Regular Season:
**67-15**
(.817)
Leading Scorer:
Michael Jordan
(30.1)

Leading Rebounder:
Horace Grant
(9.9)

Assist Leader:
Scottie Pippen
(6.9)

**PLAYOFF RESULTS:**
**Eastern Conf. First Round:**
Chicago 3, Miami 0
**Eastern Conf. Semifinals:**
Chicago 4, New York 3
**Eastern Conf. Finals:**
Chicago 4, Cleveland 2
**NBA Finals:**
Chicago 4, Portland 2

**Overall Playoff Record:**
15 Wins 7 Losses (.682)
**Overall Playoff Avg.**
**Margin of Victory:**
14.5 Points

---

### HEAD COACH: JOHN KUNDLA — 1953-54

Regular Season:
**46-26**
(.639)
Leading Scorer:
George Mikan (18.1)

Leading Rebounder:
George Mikan (14.3)

Assist Leader:
Slater Martin (3.7)

**PLAYOFF RESULTS:**
**Western Div. Round Robin**
Gm 1: Minn. 109 Rochester 88
Gm 2: Minn. 90 Fort Wayne 85
Gm 3: Minn. 78 Fort Wayne 73
Gm 4: Minn. at Rochester
(canceled)
**Western Div. Finals:**
Minneapolis 2, Rochester 1
**NBA Finals:**
Minneapolis 4, Syracuse 3

**Overall Playoff Record:**
9 Wins 4 Losses (.692)
**Playoffs Avg.**
**Margin of Victory:**
10.8 Points

### HEAD COACH: RED AUERBACH — 1960-61

Regular Season:
**57-22**
(.722)
Leading Scorer:
Tom Heinsohn
(21.3)

Leading Rebounder:
Bill Russell
(23.9)

Assist Leader:
Bob Cousy
(7.7)

**PLAYOFF RESULTS:**
**Eastern Div. Finals:**
Boston 4, Syracuse 1
**NBA Finals:**
Boston 4, St. Louis 1

**Overall Playoff Record:**
8 Wins 2 Losses (.800)
**Overall Playoff Avg.**
**Margin of Victory:**
17.1 Points

### HEAD COACH: PHIL JACKSON — 1992-93

Regular Season:
**57-25**
(.695)
Leading Scorer:
Michael Jordan
(32.6)

Leading Rebounder:
Horace Grant
(9.5)

Assist Leader:
Scottie Pippen
(6.3)

**PLAYOFF RESULTS:**
**Eastern Conf. First Round:**
Chicago 3, Atlanta 0
**Eastern Conf. Semifinals:**
Chicago 4, Cleveland 0
**Eastern Conf. Finals:**
Chicago 4, New York 2
**NBA Finals:**
Chicago 4, Phoenix 2

**Overall Playoff Record:**
15 Wins 4 Losses (.789)
**Overall Playoff Avg.**
**Margin of Victory:**
9.5 Points

---

NOTE: BOSTON WON EIGHT TITLES IN A ROW (1959–66).

# 1996-98

## CHICAGO BULLS

Overall Reg. Season Record: 203 Wins 43 Losses (.825)
Overall Playoff Record: 45 Wins 13 Losses (.776)
Overall Playoff Avg. Margin of Victory: 11.2 points

---

| HEAD COACH: PHIL JACKSON | 1995-96 |
|---|---|

**Regular Season:**

### 72-10
### (.878)

Leading Scorer:
Michael Jordan
(30.4)

Rebounder:
Dennis Rodman
(14.9)

Assist Leader:
Scottie Pippen
(5.9)

**PLAYOFF RESULTS:**

**Eastern Conf. First Round:**
Chicago 3, Miami 0
**Eastern Conf. Semifinals:**
Chicago 4, New York 1
**Eastern Conf. Finals:**
Chicago 4, Orlando 0
**NBA Finals:**
Chicago 4, Seattle 2

**Overall Playoff Record:**
15 Wins 3 Losses (.833)
**Overall Playoff Avg.**
**Margin of Victory:**
15.0 Points

---

| HEAD COACH: PHIL JACKSON | 1996-97 |
|---|---|

**Regular Season:**

### 69-13
### (.841)

Leading Scorer:
Michael Jordan
(29.6)

Leading Rebounder:
Dennis Rodman
(16.1)

Assist Leader:
Scottie Pippen
(5.7)

**PLAYOFF RESULTS:**

**Eastern Conf. First Round:**
Chicago 3, Washington 0
**Eastern Conf. Semifinals:**
Chicago 4, Atlanta 1
**Eastern Conf. Finals:**
Chicago 4, Miami 1
**NBA Finals:**
Chicago 4, Utah 2

**Overall Playoff Record:**
15 Wins 4 Losses (.789)
**Overall Playoff Avg.**
**Margin of Victory:**
7.7 Points

---

| HEAD COACH: PHIL JACKSON | 1997-98 |
|---|---|

**Regular Season:**

### 62-20
### (.756)

Leading Scorer:
Michael Jordan
(28.7)

Leading Rebounder:
Dennis Rodman
(15.0)

Assist Leader:
Scottie Pippen
(5.8)

**PLAYOFF RESULTS:**

**Eastern Conf. First Round:**
Chicago 3, New Jersey 0
**Eastern Conf. Semifinals:**
Chicago 4, Charlotte 1
**Eastern Conf. Finals:**
Chicago 4, Indiana 3
**NBA Finals:**
Chicago 4, Utah 2

**Overall Playoff Record:**
15 Wins 6 Losses (.714)
Overall Playoff Avg.
**Margin of Victory:**
10.7 Points

---

# 2000-02

## LOS ANGELES LAKERS

Overall Reg. Season Record: 181 Wins 65 Losses (.736)
Overall Playoff Record: 45 Wins 13 Losses (.775)
Overall Playoffs Avg. Margin of Victory: 10.8 Points

---

| HEAD COACH: PHIL JACKSON | 1999-2000 |
|---|---|

**Regular Season:**

### 67-15
### (.817)

Leading Scorer:
Shaquille O'Neal
(29.7)

Leading Rebounder:
Shaquille O'Neal
(13.7)

Assist Leader
Kobe Bryant
(4.9)

**PLAYOFF RESULTS:**

**Western Conf. 1st Round:**
L.A. Lakers 3, Sacramento 2
**Western Conf. Semifinals:**
L.A. Lakers 4, Phoenix 1
**Western Conf. Finals:**
L.A. Lakers 4, Portland 3
**NBA Finals:**
L.A. Lakers 4, Indiana 2

**Overall Playoff Record:**
15 Wins 8 Losses (.652)
**Overall Playoff Avg.**
**Margin of Victory:**
12.2 Points

---

| HEAD COACH: PHIL JACKSON | 2000-01 |
|---|---|

**Regular Season:**

### 56-26
### (.683)

Leading Scorer:
Shaquille O'Neal
(28.7)

Leading Rebounder:
Shaquille O'Neal
(12.7)

Assist Leader:
Kobe Bryant
(4.9)

**PLAYOFF RESULTS:**

**Western Conf. 1st Round:**
L.A. Lakers 3, Portland 0
**Western Conf. Semifinals:**
L.A. Lakers 4, Sacramento 0
**Western Conf. Finals:**
L.A. Lakers 4, San Antonio 0
**NBA Finals:**
L.A. Lakers 4, Philadelphia 1

**Overall Playoff Record:**
15 Wins 1 Loss (.938)
**Overall Playoff Avg.**
**Margin of Victory:**
14.0 Points

---

| HEAD COACH: PHIL JACKSON | 2001-02 |
|---|---|

**Regular Season:**

### 58-24
### (.707)

Leading Scorer:
Shaquille O'Neal
(27.2)

Leading Rebounder:
Shaquille O'Neal
(10.7)

Assist Leader:
Kobe Bryant
(5.5)

**PLAYOFF RESULTS:**

**Western Conf. 1st Round:**
L.A. Lakers 3, Portland 0
**Western Conf. Semifinals:**
L.A. Lakers 4, San Antonio 1
**Western Conf. Finals:**
L.A. Lakers 4, Sacramento 3
**NBA Finals:**
L.A. Lakers 4, New Jersey 0

**Overall Playoff Record:**
15 Wins 4 Losses (.789)
**Overall Playoff Avg.**
**Margin of Victory:**
6.3 Points

## DREAM MATCH-UP

RUSSELL VS. O'NEAL: THE ULTIMATE
DEFENSIVE STOPPER VERSUS TODAY'S
MOST DOMINANT OFFENSIVE FORCE.

# SHAQ

# 3

**S**uperman was lumbering but was the last to admit to any vulnerability. The kryptonite came in the form of an injured right big toe that hampered the All-Star center the entire season. Yes, the regular-season averages—27 points, 10 rebounds per game—were intact and so were the usual accolades, including another All-NBA First Team selection. But something didn't look quite right. The spin moves weren't as frequent and the explosiveness to the basket only came in flashes. Yet, as the Lakers embarked on their historic three-peat quest at the start of the playoffs, Shaquille O'Neal was the last to offer any excuses for himself or his team.

"I take all the responsibility," said O'Neal. "I've taken all the responsibility my whole career. And if something does happen, I don't want you guys [writers] to make excuses for me."

There would be no need for excuses. Only superlatives could describe the All-Star center's heroic play despite battling an assortment of injuries—sore wrist, stitched right index finger—in cementing the Lakers status as an NBA dynasty.

With L.A.'s dreams for a third championship on the brink, it was O'Neal who extended the Lakers' season with a dominating Game 6 performance in the Western Conference Finals against the Kings that forced a Game 7 in

Sacramento. Forty one points, 17 rebounds, 13 of 17 from the line. It was his best game of the postseason to date and reminiscent of the playoff domination he displayed the previous two years in L.A.'s back-to-back titles.

"He said, 'Come to me,' " said teammate Robert Horry about O'Neal's fourth-quarter performance in which he scored 12 points. "He has not said that in a long time."

It was a breakout game for a player who openly admitted earlier in the playoffs to not having his usual explosiveness to the basket.

· · · · · · · · · · · · · · · · · · · · + + + · · · · · · · · · · · · · · · · · · · ·

THE PERFORMANCE NOT ONLY GAVE THE LAKERS NEW LIFE BUT ONCE AGAIN SERVED AS A LOUD AND CLEAR REMINDER THAT WITHOUT THEIR BIG MAN WREAKING HAVOC UNDER THE BOARDS, THE LAKERS' HOPES FOR CHAMPIONSHIP SUCCESS IS GREATLY DIMINISHED. A FACT CERTAINLY NOT LOST ON HIS TEAMMATES.

· · · · · · · · · · · · · · · · · · · · + + + · · · · · · · · · · · · · · · · · · · ·

"A funny thing happened last night," said O'Neal after the Game 6 performance. "I was sleeping, with my little daughter sleeping on me. She was slobbing, I was slobbing. The phone rang about 2:30. It was Kobe. He was like, 'Big Fella, I need you tomorrow. Let's make history.'"

Not only did L.A. make history advancing past the Kings in a classic Game 7 showdown and knocking out the New Jersey Nets in the NBA Finals, but the Big Aristotle elevated his standing among basketball immortals in the process. O'Neal joined fellow greats George

Mikan of the Minneapolis Lakers and Bill Russell of the Boston Celtics as the only dominant centers to ever lead their respective teams to three championships in a row. Russell actually led the Celtics to eight in a row. While Shaq has a ways to go to reach that mark, at the age of 30, he still has a few more championships to pursue, which is certainly bad news for the rest of the league.

"There is no game plan for Shaq," said Isiah Thomas, Indiana Pacers head coach, earlier in the season. "Since I've been around basketball,

he is the only guy I've ever seen that there is no matchup for. Normally, there's a guy you can put on everybody for a matchup. But Shaq is the only guy where there is no matchup. There's not a guy in the league who can match up against him.

"There has never been a player like that. With Wilt [Chamberlain], there was Kareem [Abdul-Jabbar]. And there was Russell. But with this guy, there is nobody."

Despite O'Neal's lingering injuries in the regular season, he still managed to help lead the

Lakers to 58 wins and placed third in the MVP voting, even though he missed a total of 15 games, the most in three seasons. As Orlando Magic coach Doc Rivers pointed out when he was campaigning for Tracy McGrady in the MVP race, "Let's face it, you could vote for Shaq every year."

That's how good O'Neal is, even at 80 or 90 percent, he is still considered better than 100 percent of any player in the league, and dominant enough to lead his team to a third straight title. + + +

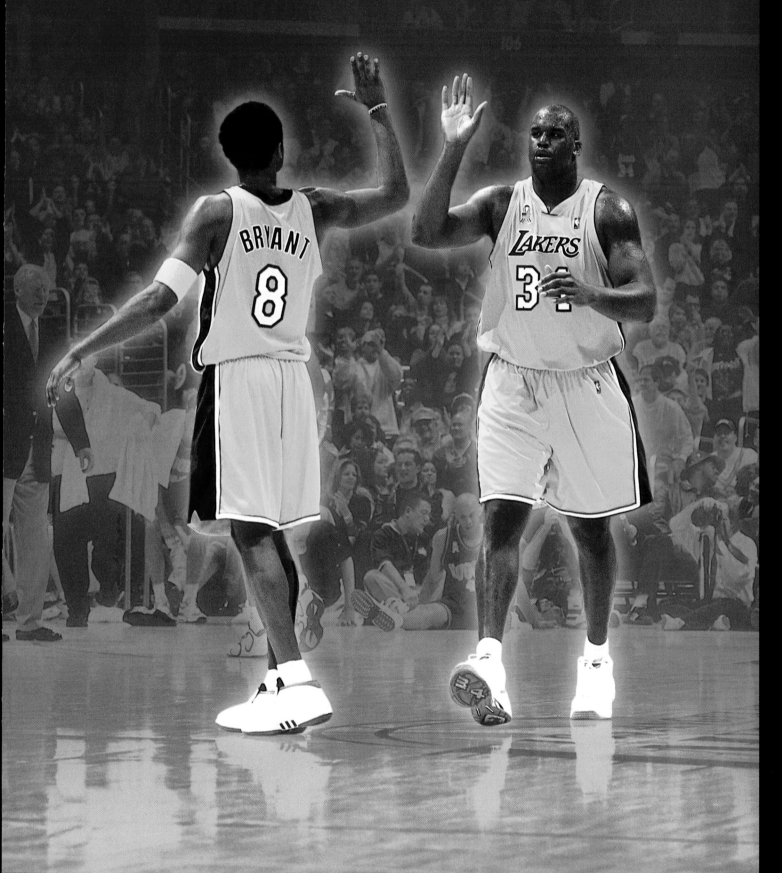

"Can't do nothing with him. Can't do anything. He's like Wilt, Kareem, Jordan, all those other guys. But Shaq is so dominant, he'll shoot 55 percent on an off night. There's nothing you can do about that. He's just going to demoralize the team. Pretty much just gonna have to deal with that." +++ KOBE BRYANT +++

# 4 KOBE

The tone was set in training camp when Shaquille O'Neal pronounced Kobe Bryant league MVP. The 1999-2000 recipient said it was time for his teammate to receive some long overdue recognition.

"I'm tired of people talking about everybody else, like Kobe doesn't exist," said O'Neal. "People talk about Michael [Jordan], Vince Carter, Tracy McGrady, those guys. Forget that. My boy is a force to be reckoned with. I'm going to be his big bully, give him a chance to run around and do what he does."

What Bryant did this season—25.2 points, 4.6 rebounds and 5.5 assists—didn't merit league MVP honors but did transcend any statistical barometer. It was a season of growth and perspective for Bryant, who evolved not only as a person but as a player. At 23 years of age, Kobe Bryant officially became a team leader.

The player once criticized for playing one on five wasn't consumed with his scoring average or his own personal highlight reel, rather this newly named co-captain embraced a team-oriented approach, involving his teammates more in the flow of the offense. The change in priorities and outlook cannot be attributed to any one lesson learned on the basketball court. It's what took place off the court that has helped transform the superstar.

"Kobe is a married man now, and a lot of responsibility comes with that," said teammate

"I'm tired of people talking about everybody else, like Kobe doesn't exist. Forget that. My boy is a force to be reckoned with. I'm going to be his big bully, give him a chance to run around and do what he does." +++ SHAQUILLE O'NEAL +++

## "Last year, I realized I had to try to make my teammates better, that was a weakness. Like any weakness, I worked on it." +++ KOBE BRYANT +++

Rick Fox. "He has the responsibility of looking outside himself. And his game has changed since his marriage. He's been very good at how he looks at his game and how he prepares for his game. But when you're in a relationship, you have to look at your partner. Now that he has the ability to do that off the court, it has made him a better player, because he is more able to work with and create for his teammates."

The maturation of Kobe Bryant was evident in the final moments of Game 3 of the First Round versus the Portland Trail Blazers. With the Lakers trailing by two points, with 10.3 seconds left in regulation, Bryant had the opportunity to be the hero. Kobe received an inbounds pass from Fox and proceeded to dribble the ball down the right side of the basket as Portland's Ruben Patterson and Scottie Pippen converged on a double team. Rather than force up a shot and potentially add to his list of game-winning heroics, Bryant dished to a wide open Robert Horry in the corner who drained the game-winning three with 2.1 seconds remaining.

"Last year Kobe wouldn't have made that pass," said Horry after the game. "He believed in himself more than this team. But all this year, he's changed."

It's difficult to pinpoint any weaknesses in a player who possesses extraordinary skill, desire and work ethic and is a perennial All-NBA and All-NBA Defensive Team selection. But if there is one aspect of his game that gnawed at Bryant, it was what made one of his childhood idols, Magic Johnson, so special.

"Last year, I realized I had to try to make my teammates better, that was a weakness," said Bryant. "Like any weakness, I worked on it."

He certainly did. Bryant took fewer shot attempts per game, which resulted in his scoring average to dip but also saw the benefits, an increase in assists. The decrease in point production didn't mean Bryant lost his zest to flash his shooter's touch every now and then.

· · · · · · · · · · · · · · · · · · + + + · · · · · · · · · · · · · · · · · ·

**WHEN SHAQ MISSED 15 GAMES DURING THE REGULAR SEASON, BRYANT SHOULDERED THE LOAD FOR L.A. IN A MID—JANUARY CONTEST AGAINST MEMPHIS, BRYANT PUT ON A SHOW, SCORING 56 POINTS IN THREE QUARTERS OF PLAY.**

· · · · · · · · · · · · · · · · · · + + + · · · · · · · · · · · · · · · · · ·

When it was apparent O'Neal wasn't quite his mobile self, it was Bryant who led the team in scoring in nine out of the 15 games leading up to the NBA Finals, including seven out of 10.

"The first year, it was all about me scoring 40 points a game for us to win," said O'Neal. "Last year, a little bit of everybody was doing it. This year, it's Kobe doing it, and I just got Kobe's back."

It seemed that the only way to potentially slow Bryant down was via room service by way of a bad bacon cheeseburger. The 6-7 guard came down with food poisoning on the eve of Game 2 of the Western Conference Finals in Sacramento, requiring three liters of intravenous fluid prior to tip off. The setback threatened to disrupt the Lakers quest for further greatness, but Kobe prevailed in the series as L.A. advanced to the Finals.

"All those cows up there and I couldn't get a decent burger?" said Bryant, delivering another dish worth savoring. + + +

"He has the responsibility of looking outside himself. And his game has changed since his marriage. He's been very good at how he looks at his game and how he prepares for his game." +++ RICK FOX +++

5 PHIL

On the eve of joining the most exclusive club in NBA coaching history, Phil Jackson was asked before the start of the NBA Finals if he was at all consumed by the challenge of winning a third straight title and a record-tying ninth overall.

"I would be in Alaska fishing," said Jackson. "I am not consumed by it. I have some down time and I am able to think about other things and enjoy my family."

The even-keeled, middle-of-the-road, Zen-like response is representative of the philosophy that has made Jackson one of the NBA's most successful coaches ever. Pressure? Jackson embraces it. When the Lakers were staring at a Game 7 do-or-die match-up in a hostile, revved-up Arco Arena against the Sacramento Kings, Jackson assembled his team that morning for one of their customary pre-game meditation sessions. *Close your eyes...Visualize happy thoughts... pure thoughts...thoughts of victory.*

Fast forward to the emotional celebration following the overtime thriller in which L.A. barely advanced to the NBA Finals.

"You can tell, the Kings finally felt the pressure," said an elated Fox talking about the play down the stretch. "For us, it was different. It was like, we were right where we wanted to be."

Jackson's ability to read a situation, on and off the court, and push the right buttons among his players was certainly put to the test this past season as the Lakers experienced a roller coaster ride in defending their NBA championship. It was a season that saw the Lakers jump out to

a 16-1 start before eventually hitting a mid-season lull and then finishing in a strong fashion—29-11 post All-Star break—as they eagerly prepared for their postseason push.

Throughout the season, Jackson challenged his players, making sure they stayed sharp for the task ahead. The Lakers marched through the first two rounds of the playoffs and appeared to have met their match in the conference finals when they were down three games to two versus Sacramento, heading to Los Angeles. With the team on the brink of elimination and thoughts of

a three-peat rapidly fading, Jackson never hit the panic button. Neither did his players.

"Coming from a military background, if the President shows no fear and the general shows no fear, usually the troops don't show any fear," said O'Neal. "Phil comes in, he's chilling. He goes through our routine and he tells us what we have to do to win. It's our job to go out there and execute it. He shows no fear. And I will never show fear, no matter what. And Kobe will never show fear no matter what. I think the guys, they feed off of that."

· · · · · · · · · · · · · · · · · · · · +++ · · · · · · · · · · · · · · · · · · · ·

**JACKSON'S ABILITY TO TURN THE PRESSURE OF THE SITUATION INTO A POSITIVE IS ONE OF HIS GREATEST STRENGTHS AS A COACH.**

· · · · · · · · · · · · · · · · · · · · +++ · · · · · · · · · · · · · · · · · · · ·

"The more the pressure's on, the more I think it's necessary to use it," said Jackson. "It develops the capacity to relax the mental brain where you have to be able to function from if you want to use decision-making abilities."

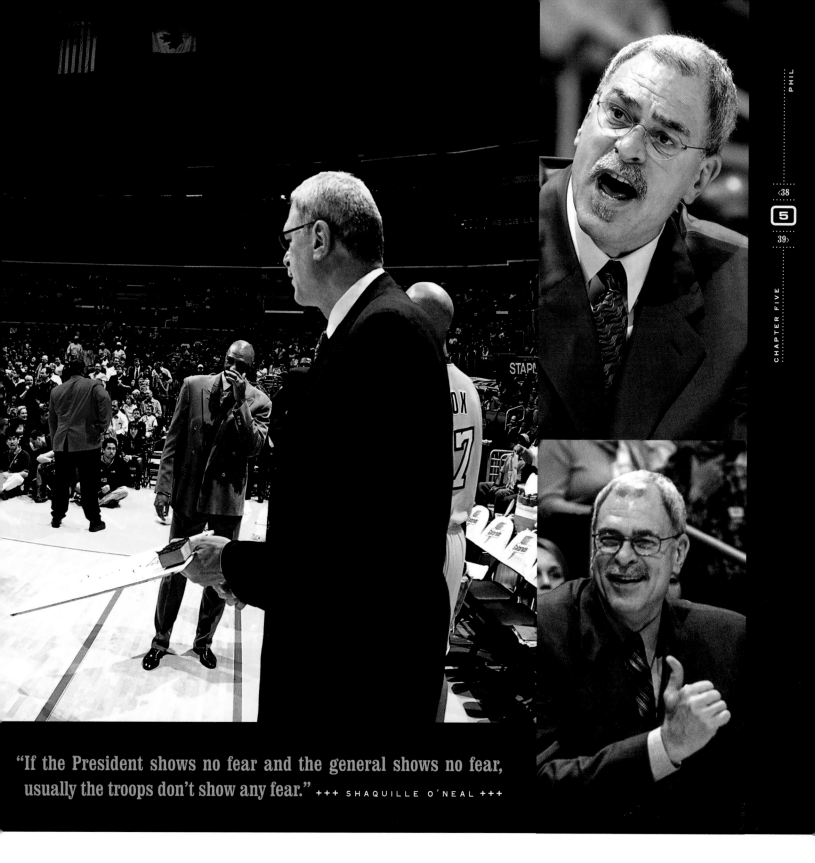

"If the President shows no fear and the general shows no fear, usually the troops don't show any fear." +++ SHAQUILLE O'NEAL +++

Jackson learned this approach first hand from one of his basketball teachers and mentors, Red Holzman, who coached the 6-8 power forward when he was with the New York Knicks. Jackson used the season he was injured—1969-70—to absorb the Hall of Famer's even-tempered approach to the game.

"I was his bench coach, the last guy in the locker room with him usually before he went on the floor," said Jackson. "He didn't have an assistant coach. He talked philosophy with me. He talked about the importance about

staying not too high, not too low and letting victory or defeats either send you tumbling one way or the other.

"He always believed in what was called the middle path. I appreciated that, his ability to handle players, particularly a team that was full of college players of the year. Cazzie Russell and Bill Bradley were both competing for the same job, but the ability for both of them to play as a team directly reflected [Holzman's] ability to handle people and make them play as a group."

The Lakers' championship adds to Jackson's sparkling résumé. Not only did he tie legendary Red Auerbach for the most NBA championships— nine—but Jackson also surpassed Pat Riley as the all-time playoff leader in victories with 156. The Zen Master has now coached two separate franchises to three-peats, twice with Chicago and now with L.A., and has not lost a playoff series dating back to 1995, translating into 24 straight, the most in NBA history.

It's certainly a lot for Jackson to ponder on his next fishing trip. + + +

## NBA CHAMPIONSHIPS

PHIL JACKSON, CHICAGO BULLS, LOS ANGELES LAKERS
9 › RED AUERBACH, BOSTON CELTICS
5 › JOHN KUNDLA, MINNEAPOLIS LAKERS
4 › PAT RILEY, LOS ANGELES LAKERS

# 9

### Most Career NBA Playoff Coaching Victories

| COACH | W–L | PCT |
|---|---|---|
| PHIL JACKSON › | 156–54 | .743 |
| PAT RILEY › | 155–100 | .608 |
| RED AUERBACH › | 99–69 | .589 |
| K.C. JONES › | 81–57 | .587 |
| LENNY WILKENS › | 80–94 | .460 |
| JERRY SLOAN › | 77–76 | .503 |
| CHUCK DALY › | 75–51 | .595 |
| BILLY CUNNINGHAM › | 66–39 | .629 |
| LARRY BROWN › | 63–66 | .488 |
| JOHN KUNDLA › | 60–35 | .632 |

## CAREER NBA PLAYOFF COACHING VICTORIES

# 156-54

**(.743) HIGHEST ALL-TIME NBA PLAYOFF WINNING PCT.**

# 24

## CONSECUTIVE NBA PLAYOFF SERIES WON

THE NUMBER OF CONSECUTIVE NBA PLAYOFF SERIES WON BY A PHIL JACKSON COACHED TEAM. THE LAST TIME JACKSON LOST A PLAYOFF SERIES DATES BACK TO 1995 WHEN HE WAS COACH OF THE CHICAGO BULLS. THE ORLANDO MAGIC DEFEATED THE BULLS IN THE EASTERN CONFERENCE SEMIFINALS (4–2).

# 60.5

## AVERAGE NUMBER OF NBA REGULAR-SEASON WINS IN 12 SEASONS

### Highest All-Time NBA Regular-Season Winning Percentage

| PCT. | W | L |
|---|---|---|
| .738 | 726 | 258 |

**T**hey toil in the shadows. The spotlight shines on them infrequently yet they are essential to the Los Angeles Lakers' championship success. They are the role players. A group of invaluable contributors who rise to the occasion, time and time again. Double up on Shaq and Kobe and they'll make you pay from the perimeter. Go single coverage on the All-Stars and the results are even more damaging.

"If you stay home with the supporting cast, then Shaq's going to go for 40 and Kobe's going to go for 40," said Rick Fox, one of the key contributors in L.A.'s three title teams. "So as you pick your poison, it's going to be a tossup. It's difficult, because we're confident enough to find ways to be effective."

Effective may be an understatement. How about season-saving? The "supporting cast" may have had its ups and downs throughout the season as the team worked in three new key additions—

Mitch Richmond, Samaki Walker and Lindsey Hunter—but no one's contribution to the team loomed larger than Robert Horry's heroics in Game 4 of the Western Conference Finals. It was Horry's long-range shot attempt—not Shaq or Kobe's—that carried the dynastic hopes and dreams of everyone in the L.A. metropolitan area.

"That ball in the air represented our season," said Derek Fisher.

With six-tenths of a second left in regulation,

# SUPPORTING CAST 6

Horry hit a 25-foot top-of-the-key game winner against the Sacramento Kings that gave L.A. a season-saving victory, a 2-2 series tie and a demoralizing loss for the Kings.

"He has a steel kind of will," said Lakers head coach Phil Jackson about Horry's penchant for saving the day.

Laker fans have grown accustomed to Horry's late-game heroics. Who could forget his clutch shooting in Game 3 of last season's NBA Finals against Philadelphia when he nailed a three with 47 seconds left to seal L.A.'s victory when the series was tied at one game apiece? Or the three

While Horry has carved a reputation as one of the all-time great playoff clutch shooters in NBA history, Fisher has shown his own ability as L.A.'s other money role player, especially during the NBA Finals. Fisher, who shared time at the point guard position in the regular season with Lindsey Hunter, shot a sizzling 66.7 (8 for 12) from beyond the three-point line against the New Jersey Nets.

"I think those shots really opened up Shaq's game," said Fisher, whose three-point totals from the last three NBA Finals—25 for 43—is an impressive 58 percent. "They just couldn't put everyone on him."

Samaki Walker, who amid last summer, had the daunting task of starting at the power forward position for a two-time world champion team. Walker started 63 games at that position, including 15 at the center spot in place of O'Neal when he was sidelined. Walker averaged 7.0 rebounds a game and came off the bench for the Lakers in the latter stages of the postseason and helped attack the boards.

Although he only started one regular-season game, Devean George provided a spark for the Lakers off the bench, posting career highs across the board, including minutes (21.5) and points per

DEREK FISHER          SAMAKI WALKER                    ROBERT HORRY

STANISLAV MEDVEDENKO                                    RICK FOX

from the corner with 2.1 seconds left against Portland in the first round that slammed the door on the Trail Blazers' season and completed the sweep?

"Basically, I'm not a superstar; I'm not a little star," said Horry, who hit several clutch baskets throughout the 2002 postseason. "I'm just a guy that nobody pays a lot of attention to, so when the ball comes to me, I just let it go. If I make it, big deal. I look good. If I miss it, it's like, 'Why is he taking that shot anyway?' I don't worry about it. I just take the shot because it's there."

Fox, one of the team's co-captains along with Shaq and Kobe, once again showed how valuable his veteran leadership and contributions are to the team. The 6-7 forward, who averaged 7.9 points and shot .313 from the three-point line during the regular season, raised his scoring average (9.8) and shooting percentage (.522) when the team needed him the most, in the Finals.

Brian Shaw, another veteran player, didn't post big numbers in the regular season or playoffs, but his understanding of the Triangle Offense and leadership belied any stat sheet.

game (7.1) and came up big in Games 3 and 4 of the Finals, hitting clutch shots and grabbing key rebounds.

Veteran shooting guard Mitch Richmond's season did not go according to expectation. He averaged only 11.1 minutes and 4.1 points per game. Despite seeing limited playing time, the 14-year player and six time All-Star did receive his coveted NBA championship ring.

"The guys played well all year," said Richmond, who played in the final minute of Game 4 of the Finals. "I didn't play as much as I wanted to, but

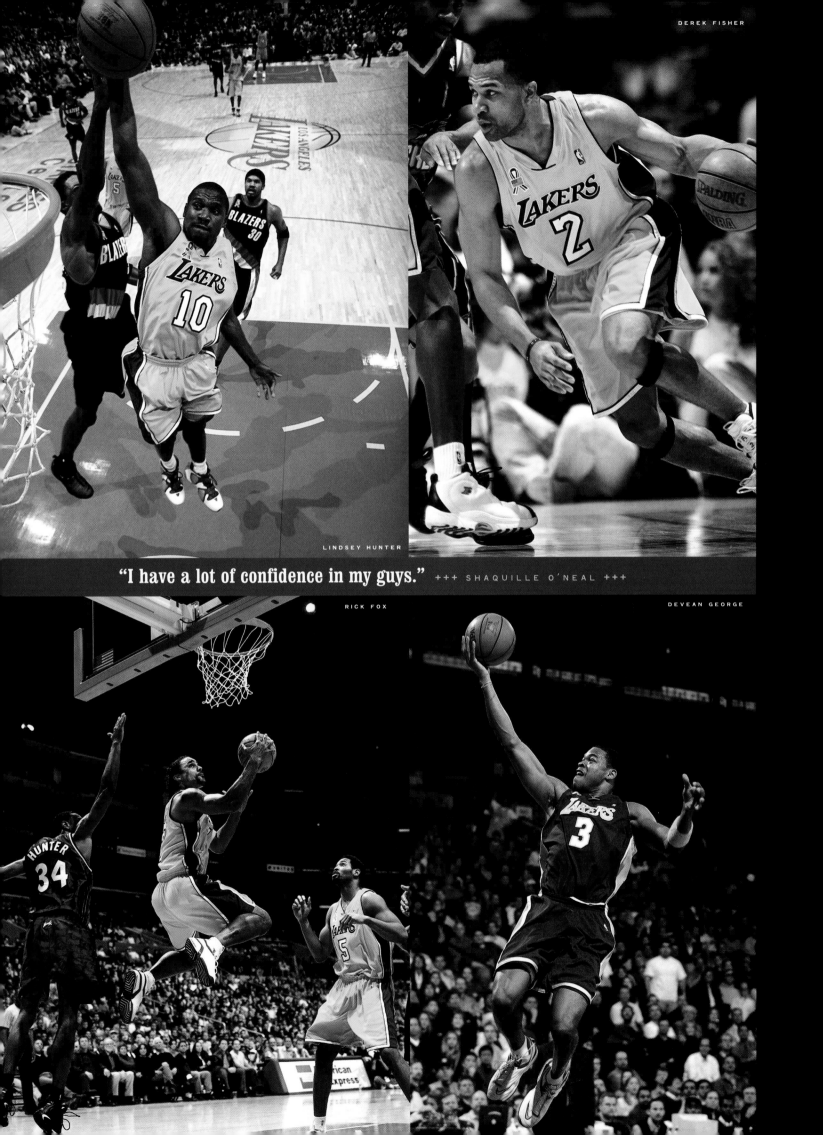

DEREK FISHER

LINDSEY HUNTER

"I have a lot of confidence in my guys." +++ SHAQUILLE O'NEAL +++

RICK FOX

DEVEAN GEORGE

BRIAN SHAW

"I'm not a superstar; I'm not a little star. I'm just a guy that nobody pays a lot of attention to." +++ ROBERT HORRY +++

MARK MADSEN

JELANI McCOY    MITCH RICHMOND

" If you stay home with the supporting cast, then Shaq's going to go for 40 and Kobe's going to go for 40." +++ RICK FOX +++

MARK MADSEN AND
LINDSEY HUNTER

BRIAN SHAW AND
SHAQUILLE O'NEAL

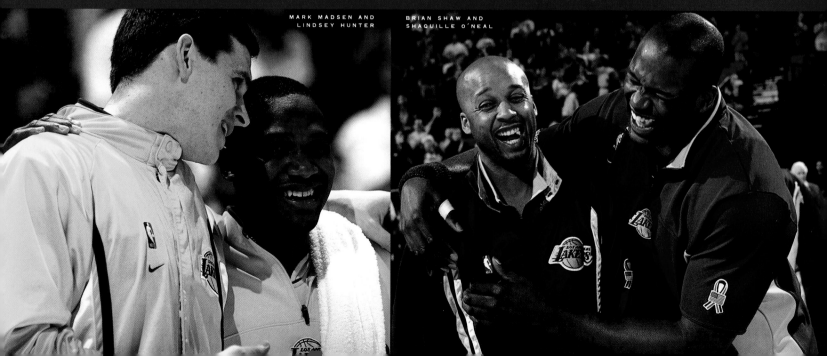

ROBERT HORRY

it's still one of the best seasons for me. This is what it's all about. It's a great feeling. You never know how you're going to feel, but being in there at the end of the game was nice. Just being a part of it."

Lindsey Hunter, who was acquired just prior to the season, started 47 games at point guard and provided the team with added insurance at that position, especially when Fisher missed the first 12 games recovering from offseason surgery.

Other contributors throughout the season included power forwards Stanislav Medvedenko and Mark Madsen, who averaged 10.3 and 11.0 minutes, respectively, per game while Jelani McCoy saw action in 21 games.

For Horry, Fisher, Shaw and Fox, key contributors on three championship teams, their names may not shine as bright as their more celebrated teammates, Shaq and Kobe, but they're officially part of the Lakers' championship lore.

"In past eras and championship teams, some of the role players were the favorite guys," said Fisher. "The Kurt Rambises, Michael Coopers, Norm Nixons and other guys. Year after year, it was those guys that people had a lot of respect for even though other guys got a lot of the credit. I think it's going to be hopefully the same for us, as we continue to be part of something special." + + +

**T**he two-time defending champions were sticking their chests out. It was early December and the challenge for most regular-season victories was before them.

"I think we can do it," said Kobe Bryant of reaching 73 regular-season wins, one more than the 1995-96 Chicago Bulls' record of 72-10. "I know we can do it. It's a matter of going out and doing it."

Bryant's confidence was understandable. In pursuit of their third consecutive title, the Lakers jumped out of the regular-season gate with a franchise best 16-1 record as Bryant and his coach, Phil Jackson, picked up Player and Coach of the Month honors for November.

"I don't think there's any question we have the talent to do so," added Bryant. "We have the best team in the league. Put aside Shaq, put aside myself. We still have the team. We want to play together. We enjoy playing together."

The air of invincibility didn't last, as the Lakers finished the month of December with a 7-5 record. Shaquille O'Neal was shelved for five games, having been placed on the injured list with an arthritic big right toe. Suddenly, thoughts of the regular-season record faded as the surging Sacramento Kings were closing the gap on the first-place Lakers in the Pacific Division. To make matters worse, for 13 days in February, O'Neal was once again sidelined due to

# 7
# THE SEASON

WITH SHAQ ON THE SIDELINES FOR 15 GAMES, THE LAKERS WENT 7–8. "YOU DON'T WANT TO SAY THAT WE'RE A MEDIOCRE TEAM WITHOUT SHAQ, BUT THAT'S REALLY WHAT WE ARE," SAID RICK FOX.

+ + +

soreness in his toe. The injury would hinder him the rest of the season.

The Lakers, who welcomed new additions to their roster, most notably Mitch Richmond, Samaki Walker and Lindsey Hunter, entered the All-Star break with a 33-13 record and last season's regular-season and NBA Finals MVP on the bench in street clothes. The regular-season march did hit a few speed bumps along the way, as the Lakers lost to the lottery-bound Memphis Grizzlies, Chicago Bulls (twice!) and Denver Nuggets.

"We've messed around, didn't make shots, didn't come ready, and teams are pumped up," said O'Neal reflecting on the first half of the season during All-Star weekend in Philadelphia. "They're playing L.A., they're jumping up and down. However, I've been playing for the Lakers six years, and every now and then, you lose a game. So either we can blame it on one of those nights, or we just don't get up for teams like they get up for us. We'll be fine. I like where we're at. Other teams are playing their best, we're not playing our best,

and we're still right at the top. So we have the ability to turn it on when we need to, and we will."

......................... + + + .........................

TRUE TO SHAQ'S WORDS, THE LAKERS REGAINED FOCUS AND FORM, POSTING A 29— 11 RECORD AFTER THE ALL-STAR BREAK, CLEARLY RAISING THEIR LEVEL OF PLAY.

......................... + + + .........................

"This time of year you start to anticipate the emotion level that's part of late-season

## WELCOME BACK, CHICK!

• • • • • • • • • • • • • • ✦ ✦ ✦ • • • • • • • • • • • • • •

CHICK HEARN, THE LAKERS' LEGENDARY BROADCASTER, SAW HIS
INCREDIBLE STREAK OF 3,338 CONSECUTIVE GAMES BROADCAST END
DECEMBER 20, 2001. THE 85–YEAR–OLD HAD TO UNDERGO OPEN–HEART
SURGERY TO REPLACE A VALVE. IT WAS THE FIRST GAME HE HAD MISSED
SINCE NOVEMBER 20, 1965, WHEN BAD WEATHER GROUNDED HIM FROM
FLYING TO HIS NEXT DESTINATION. THE BROADCASTING LEGEND ALSO
UNDERWENT HIP SURGERY AND FINALLY RETURNED, TO THE DELIGHT OF
SOUTHERN CALIFORNIANS EVERYWHERE, ON APRIL 9, 2002 WHEN HE
CALLED THE LAKERS' 30–POINT VICTORY OVER THE UTAH JAZZ.

• • • • • • • • • • • • • • ✦ ✦ ✦ • • • • • • • • • • • • • •

and postseason action," said Derek Fisher, who missed the first 12 games of the season recovering from offseason surgery on his right foot.

The Combo, O'Neal and Bryant, of course, led the way for L.A. O'Neal averaged 27.2 points and 10.7 rebounds for the season while Bryant averaged 25.2 points, 5.5 rebounds and 5.5 assists. The Lakers still were chasing the Kings, who were on track for their best regular-season record in franchise history.

"The regular season, if we wind up having home-court advantage, that is great," Bryant said. "But if we don't, that's fine, too. But when the playoffs start, the title has to come through L.A. I don't care what your record is."

Despite L.A.'s second-half push, the Kings won the Pacific Division with a 61-21 record and did secure home-court advantage throughout the playoffs. Home-court advantage or not, the Lakers couldn't afford to be without O'Neal, who ended up missing 15 regular-

season games, in their quest for a third consecutive title. The Lakers were 7-8 without the Big Aristotle in the lineup and 51-16 with him patrolling the lane. All eyes were on Shaq as the postseason drew near.

"I'll have new adrenaline, new enthusiasm and emotion in the playoffs," said O'Neal. "It only takes 15 wins. The first team to win 15 games is the champion." ✦ ✦ ✦

DEREK FISHER

## MVP! MVP!

KOBE BRYANT STOLE THE ALL-STAR SHOW IN HIS HOMETOWN OF PHILADELPHIA WITH A 31-POINT EFFORT IN LEADING THE WEST TO A 135–120 VICTORY. "HE WAS A STEP AHEAD OF THE BEST IN THE LEAGUE, AND YOU COULD SEE IT," SAID DON NELSON, HEAD COACH OF THE WEST. "THAT'S HARD TO DO, BECAUSE THERE WERE SOME GREAT, GREAT PLAYERS OUT THERE."

LINDSEY HUNTER

STANISLAV MEDVEDENKO [14]
AND DEVEAN GEORGE [3]

8 POST

# SEASON

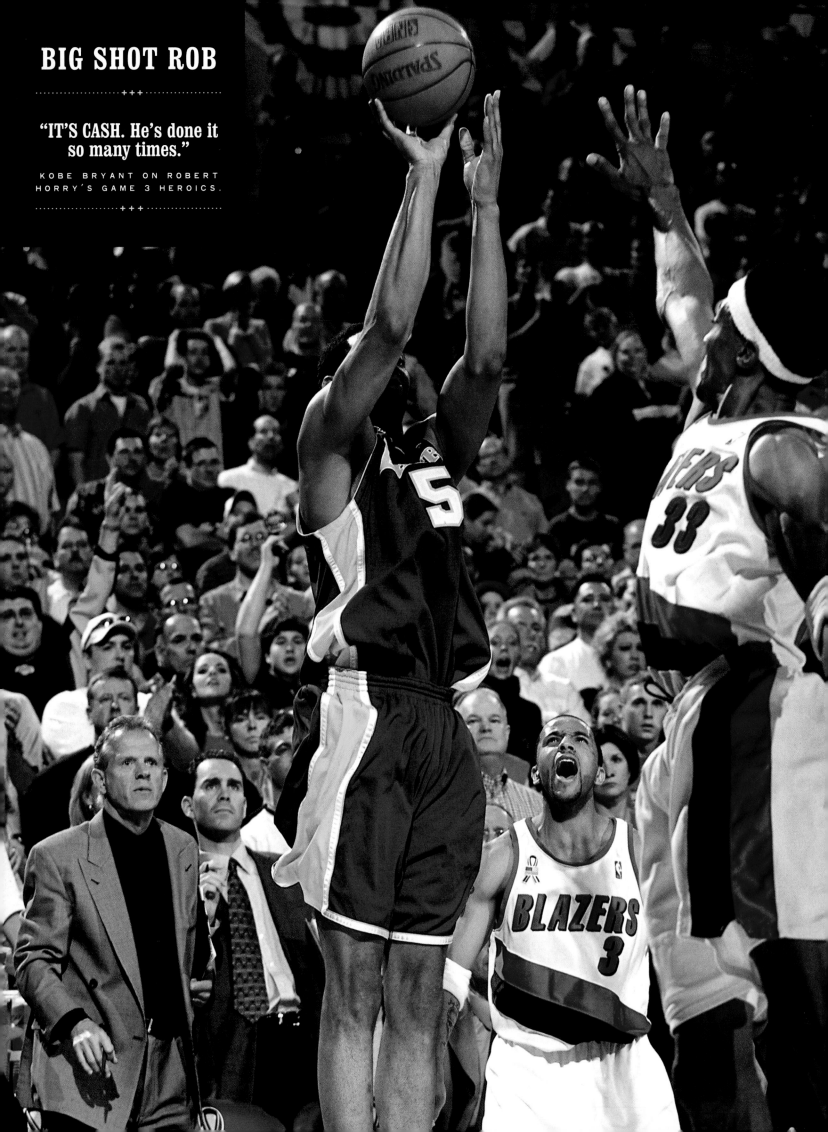

# BIG SHOT ROB

+++

"IT'S CASH. He's done it so many times."

KOBE BRYANT ON ROBERT HORRY'S GAME 3 HEROICS.

+++

# Portland

**T**he official three-peat quest began against the Portland Trail Blazers, a team the Lakers faced in the postseason during their last two championship runs. After jumping out to a two games to none lead, the Lakers were looking to close out the series at the Rose Garden. But the Blazers were hoping to avoid a second consecutive postseason sweep to the NBA champions.

It appeared the Blazers would get their wish as the team led by five points with 39 seconds remaining in regulation. Yet, similar to their Game 7 collapse in the 2000 Western Conference Finals, the Blazers couldn't hold on to the lead. Portland led by two with seconds remaining as Kobe Bryant drove to the basket and

LOS ANGELES ›

# 3

PORTLAND ›

# 0

dished the ball to a wide open Robert Horry, who drained a three from the corner with 2.1 seconds remaining.

"Did I want the ball? No, I was kind of scared," said Horry afterwards. "I just threw it up there, and I didn't know if it was going in or out."

For the Blazers, it was yet another bitter playoff defeat to their Pacific Division rivals.

"We played our hearts out," said Portland swingman Bonzi Wells. "Everybody came out here and left it all on the court, but they're the world champs. And we're just like all the rest of the teams in the league. We're just fighting for second." + + +

**4** ‹ LOS ANGELES

**1**

SAN ANTONIO ›

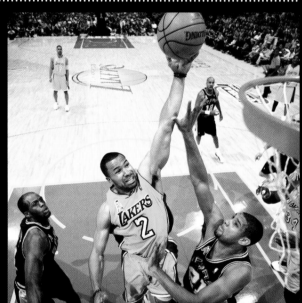

F resh off their sweep of the Portland Trail Blazers, the Lakers were on a roll, having won 19 out of their last 20 playoff games dating back to last season. Make that 20 out of 21 as L.A. upended the San Antonio Spurs in Game 1 of the Western Conference Semifinals. Shaquille O'Neal, who was hampered with an arthritic right big toe, experienced a few other injuries in this series, so it was up to Kobe Bryant to shoulder the scoring load for L.A. The Lakers ended up dropping the second game of the series as Tim Duncan scored 27 points and pulled down 17 rebounds.

"It's huge for us, we really needed this one," said Duncan, whose frontcourtmate, David Robinson, missed the first three games due to a sore back. "It was a semi-

must win. We wanted to come in here and take one. We're right where we want to be."

The positive vibes didn't last long for the Spurs as the Lakers regained their stride and disposed of San Antonio in the next three games behind Bryant's 28.3 points-per-game average.

"It's another frustrating defeat at the hands of the Lakers," said Spurs forward, Malik Rose, whose team was outscored 125-88 in the fourth quarter of the series. "We played them the best they can be played. It's going to be a pretty depressing couple of weeks." + + +

# San Antonio

WESTERN CONFERENCE SEMIFINALS

# Sacramento

------------------------------------------- WESTERN CONFERENCE FINALS

he series was an instant classic, filled with drama, emerging heroes and plenty of clutch shooting. Two heavyweights exchanging blows until both could barely stand. The challenger, Sacramento Kings, had the two-time NBA champion Los Angeles Lakers on the ropes, but were unable to deliver the final knockout punch. The Kings were seconds away from enjoying a commanding three games to one lead when L.A. delivered a right jab of their own in the form of a Robert Horry three-pointer from the top of the key. The buzzer-beater gave the Lakers new life, tying the series two games apiece.

"That's a victory from the jaws of defeat," said Lakers head coach Phil Jackson.

What ensued were three of the most thrilling playoff games in recent memory that fittingly went down to the wire. The climactic Game 7 in Arco Arena saw a series of heart-pounding

LOS ANGELES ›

4

SACRAMENTO ›

3

lead changes down the stretch as Sacramento rode its new money player, point guard Mike Bibby, who scored 10 of the team's final 12 points in regulation. The seesaw game went into overtime but the Lakers championship experience proved too much for the Kings.

"They played us well all season, they played us well during the series, they thought it was their time," said O'Neal, who scored 35 points in Game 7. "But it wasn't." + + +

"I have so much respect for him. That's the most fun I've ever had against anyone I've played against." +++ KOBE BRYANT ON MIKE BIBBY +++

2002 Destiny >
vs.

< Dynasty

99 ⟨ LOS ANGELES

O { DESTINY } DYNASTY } 1

NEW JERSEY ⟩ 94

JUNE 5, 2002

# GAME
# 1234

# "The best way to defeat him is to figure out what car he's going to drive and put sand in the gas tank. If he makes it to the arena, we're going to be in trouble."

### +++ **Jason Kidd** +++

**T**he buildup prior to tipoff of Game 1 centered on the perceived gap between the two franchises. The two-time defending NBA champions, Los Angeles Lakers, physically and emotionally spent from slugging it out against their equally matched opponent, the Sacramento Kings in the Western Conference Finals, had overcome their most difficult hurdle yet. The skies had now opened. It was a mere formality that the Lakers would be crowned champions.

After all, how could the New Jersey Nets and their first place record of 52-30 in the airtight Eastern Conference matchup with Shaq, Kobe and the Lakers from the dominant Western Conference, where they would rank fifth overall in the seedings? The second the overtime buzzer sounded in Game 7 in Sacramento on Sunday night, the Nets were listed as overwhelming underdogs.

"It seems like everything we did in the regular season didn't matter," said Nets head coach Byron Scott. "We've been underdogs in the last two series. Charlotte was supposed to beat us. Boston was supposed to beat us.

"I think our guys enjoy the fact that everybody is not picking us. I know we are the biggest underdogs in the history of the NBA Finals."

After 12 minutes of play in Game 1, the label seemed to suit New Jersey. The Lakers took control of the game early, overpowering the Nets, who appeared uncomfortable and passive under the bright lights of the NBA Finals stage, as Shaq led the offensive attack with 10 points, three blocks and three rebounds en route to a 29-14 lead.

The gap grew as wide as 23 points before New Jersey shook off the jitters and played with a greater focus as L.A. seemed to lose theirs.

Jason Kidd led the Nets with a triple-double, the 26th in NBA Finals history, and helped bring his team to within three points. But the Nets couldn't break through, as Shaq tapped into his championship experience by scoring eight points down the stretch to seal the victory.

"We're confident that we can play with these guys," said Keith Van Horn, whose Nets made only 15 out of 26 free throws (57.7) for the game. "We just need to do it for four quarters and come out with more fire. We just kind of were asleep in the first quarter."

Over in the Los Angeles locker room, head coach Phil Jackson scribbled a message on the chalk-board that summed up the Lakers mood: "We gave them confidence. Let's take it back." + + +

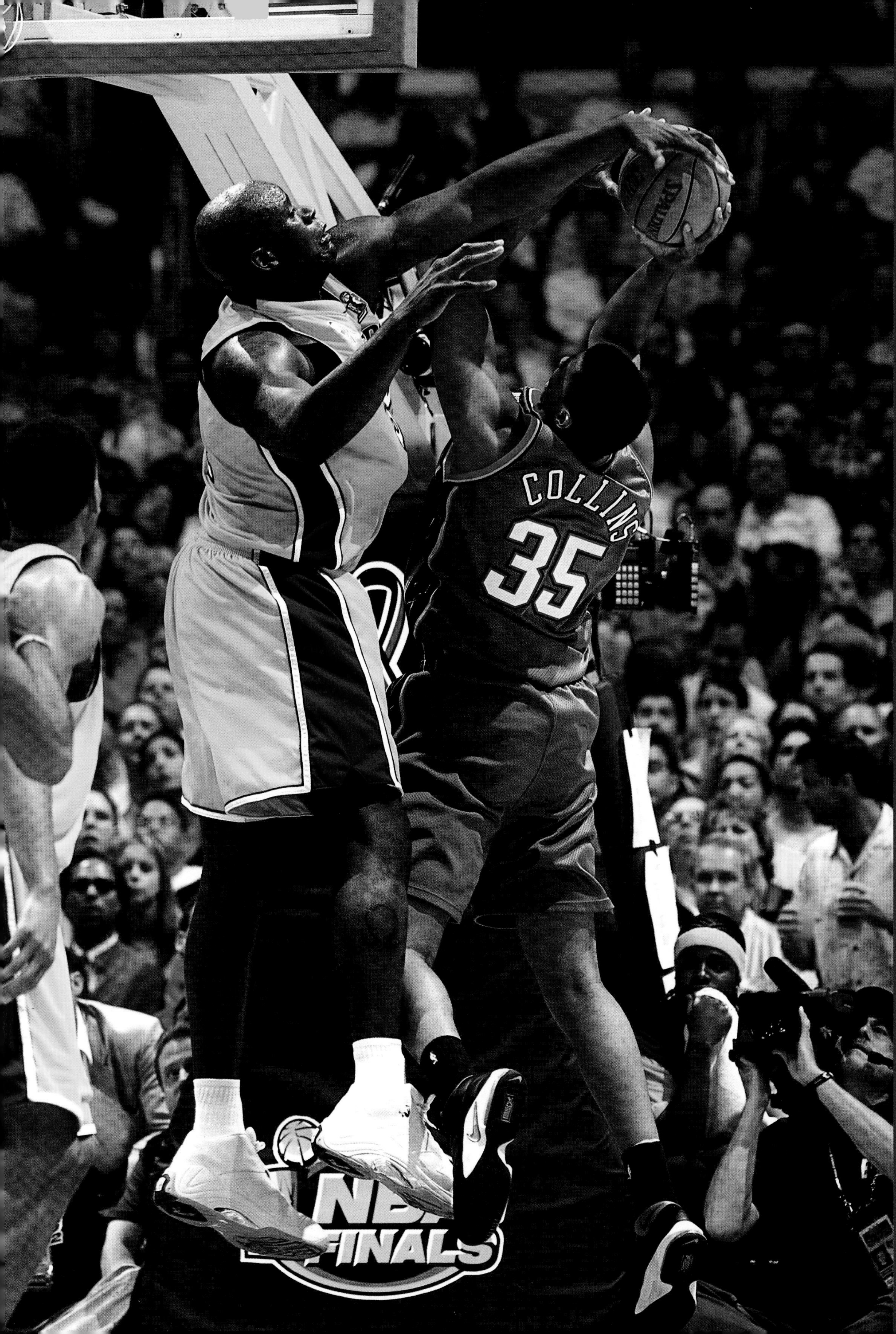
COLLINS
35
NBA FINALS

JASON KIDD AND THE NETS STUMBLED OUT OF THE GATE IN THE FIRST QUARTER OF GAME 1, FALLING BEHIND BY 15 POINTS BEFORE MAKING THEIR VALIANT COMEBACK. THE NETS OUTSCORED L.A. 80–70 OVER THE LAST THREE QUARTERS. "THIS GIVES US A LOT OF CONFIDENCE," SAID KIDD, WHO RECORDED A TRIPLE-DOUBLE. "WE DIDN'T GIVE UP. WE KNOCKED ON THE DOOR, BUT WE DIDN'T COME THROUGH. THROW THE FIRST QUARTER OUT THE WINDOW AND THAT'S THE TEAM THAT NEEDS TO COME OUT FOR FOUR QUARTERS [FRIDAY]."

Mitch Richmond and Shaquille O'Neal had plenty to smile about at the end of Game 1, while Phil Jackson wasn't pleased by his team's let down as Byron Scott and the Nets threatened to pull off the upset. "I thought [the Lakers] played in cruise control," said Jackson. "The Nets got some momentum and [it] got them back in the ballgame."

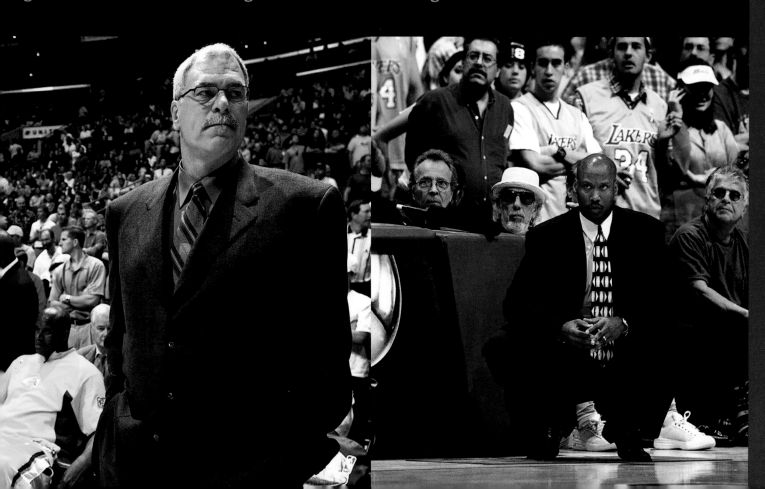

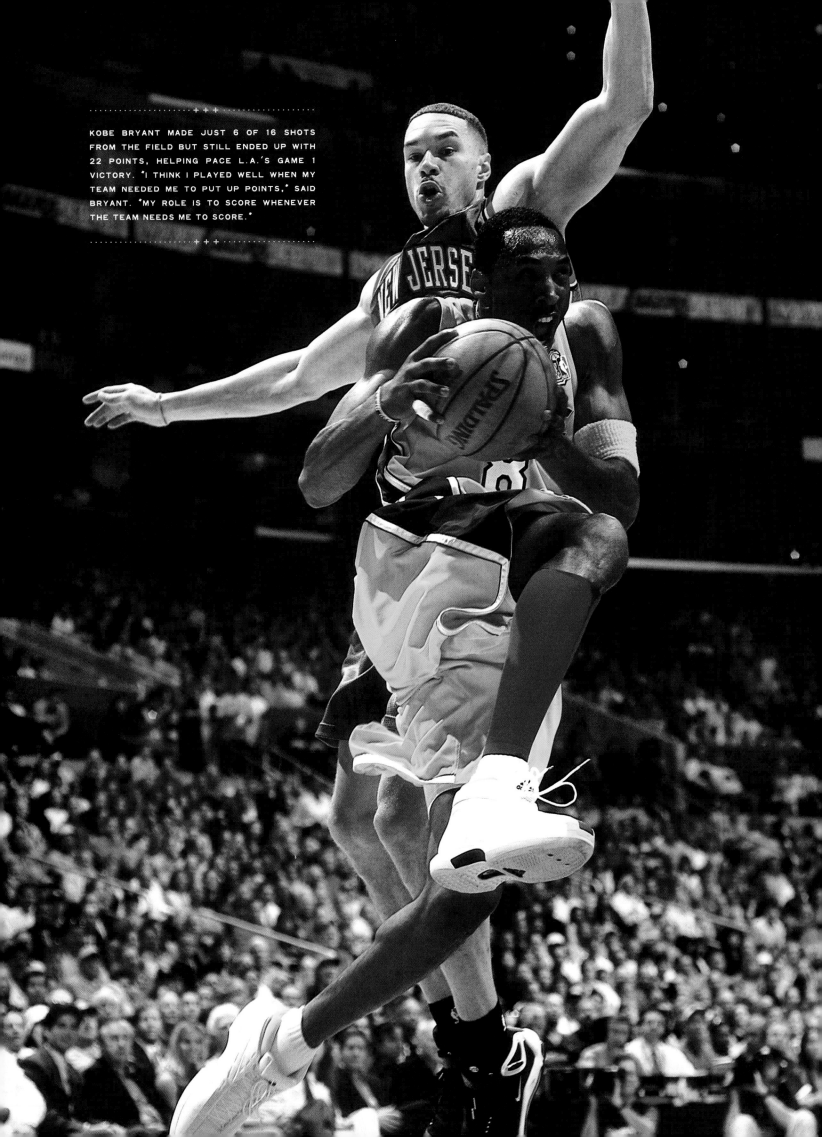

KOBE BRYANT MADE JUST 6 OF 16 SHOTS FROM THE FIELD BUT STILL ENDED UP WITH 22 POINTS, HELPING PACE L.A.'S GAME 1 VICTORY. "I THINK I PLAYED WELL WHEN MY TEAM NEEDED ME TO PUT UP POINTS," SAID BRYANT. "MY ROLE IS TO SCORE WHENEVER THE TEAM NEEDS ME TO SCORE."

## NEW JERSEY NETS

| PLAYER | POS | MIN | FGM-A | 3GM-A | FTM-A | REBOUNDS OFF | DEF | TOT | AST | PF | ST | TO | BS | PTS |
|---|---|---|---|---|---|---|---|---|---|---|---|---|---|---|
| JASON KIDD | G | 43 | 11-26 | 1-3 | 0-1 | 6 | 4 | 10 | 10 | 1 | 3 | 1 | 0 | 23 |
| KERRY KITTLES | G | 25 | 3-7 | 1-2 | 2-2 | 0 | 0 | 0 | 1 | 1 | 0 | 1 | 1 | 9 |
| KENYON MARTIN | F | 37 | 7-22 | 1-3 | 6-9 | 3 | 3 | 6 | 2 | 3 | 0 | 3 | 1 | 21 |
| KEITH VAN HORN | F | 35 | 5-14 | 2-6 | 0-0 | 2 | 4 | 6 | 1 | 6 | 0 | 4 | 0 | 12 |
| TODD MACCULLOCH | C | 25 | 5-9 | 0-0 | 0-2 | 6 | 2 | 8 | 0 | 3 | 2 | 2 | 1 | 10 |
| Lucious Harris | + | 25 | 1-5 | 0-2 | 3-4 | 1 | 2 | 3 | 2 | 3 | 0 | 0 | 0 | 5 |
| Richard Jefferson | + | 22 | 2-4 | 0-0 | 0-2 | 0 | 6 | 6 | 1 | 3 | 1 | 0 | 0 | 4 |
| Aaron Williams | + | 15 | 2-5 | 0-0 | 0-0 | 1 | 3 | 4 | 1 | 4 | 3 | 0 | 1 | 4 |
| Jason Collins | + | 8 | 1-1 | 0-0 | 3-4 | 2 | 0 | 2 | 1 | 5 | 0 | 0 | 0 | 5 |
| Anthony Johnson | + | 5 | 0-1 | 0-0 | 1-2 | 0 | 0 | 0 | 0 | 0 | 0 | 0 | 0 | 1 |
| Donny Marshall | + | DNP | + | + | + | + | + | + | + | + | + | + | + | + |
| Brian Scalabrine | + | DNP | + | + | + | + | + | + | + | + | + | + | + | + |
| TOTAL | | 240 | 37-94 | 5-16 | 15-26 | 21 | 24 | 45 | 19 | 29 | 9 | 11 | 4 | 94 |
| | | | (39.4) | (31.3) | (57.7) | Team Rebs: 15 | | | | | | | | |

## LOS ANGELES LAKERS

| PLAYER | POS | MIN | FGM-A | 3GM-A | FTM-A | REBOUNDS OFF | DEF | TOT | AST | PF | ST | TO | BS | PTS |
|---|---|---|---|---|---|---|---|---|---|---|---|---|---|---|
| KOBE BRYANT | G | 43 | 6-16 | 0-2 | 10-11 | 1 | 2 | 3 | 6 | 2 | 1 | 4 | 0 | 22 |
| DEREK FISHER | G | 36 | 4-7 | 1-2 | 4-4 | 0 | 1 | 1 | 2 | 1 | 1 | 2 | 0 | 13 |
| ROBERT HORRY | F | 41 | 2-6 | 0-2 | 1-2 | 1 | 7 | 8 | 4 | 2 | 3 | 0 | 2 | 5 |
| RICK FOX | F | 39 | 5-8 | 0-1 | 4-6 | 5 | 3 | 8 | 3 | 5 | 2 | 2 | 0 | 14 |
| SHAQUILLE O'NEAL | C | 40 | 12-22 | 0-0 | 12-21 | 2 | 14 | 16 | 1 | 2 | 1 | 5 | 4 | 36 |
| Brian Shaw | + | 11 | 0-2 | 0-1 | 0-0 | 2 | 0 | 2 | 5 | 2 | 0 | 0 | 1 | 0 |
| Devean George | + | 11 | 1-5 | 0-1 | 1-1 | 1 | 2 | 3 | 0 | 2 | 0 | 1 | 0 | 3 |
| Samaki Walker | + | 8 | 1-2 | 0-0 | 0-0 | 3 | 4 | 7 | 0 | 1 | 0 | 2 | 1 | 2 |
| Lindsey Hunter | + | 6 | 1-3 | 0-1 | 0-0 | 1 | 0 | 1 | 0 | 2 | 0 | 0 | 0 | 2 |
| Stanislav Medvedenko | + | 5 | 1-1 | 0-0 | 0-0 | 1 | 0 | 1 | 0 | 1 | 0 | 0 | 0 | 2 |
| Mark Madsen | + | DNP | + | + | + | + | + | + | + | + | + | + | + | + |
| Mitch Richmond | + | DNP | + | + | + | + | + | + | + | + | + | + | + | + |
| TOTAL | | 240 | 33-72 | 1-10 | 32-45 | 17 | 33 | 50 | 21 | 20 | 8 | 16 | 8 | 99 |
| | | | (45.8) | (10.0) | (71.1) | Team Rebs: 10 | | | | | | | | |

"WE JUST HAVE TO RELAX. NOBODY SAID IT WAS GOING TO BE EASY." +++ JASON KIDD +++

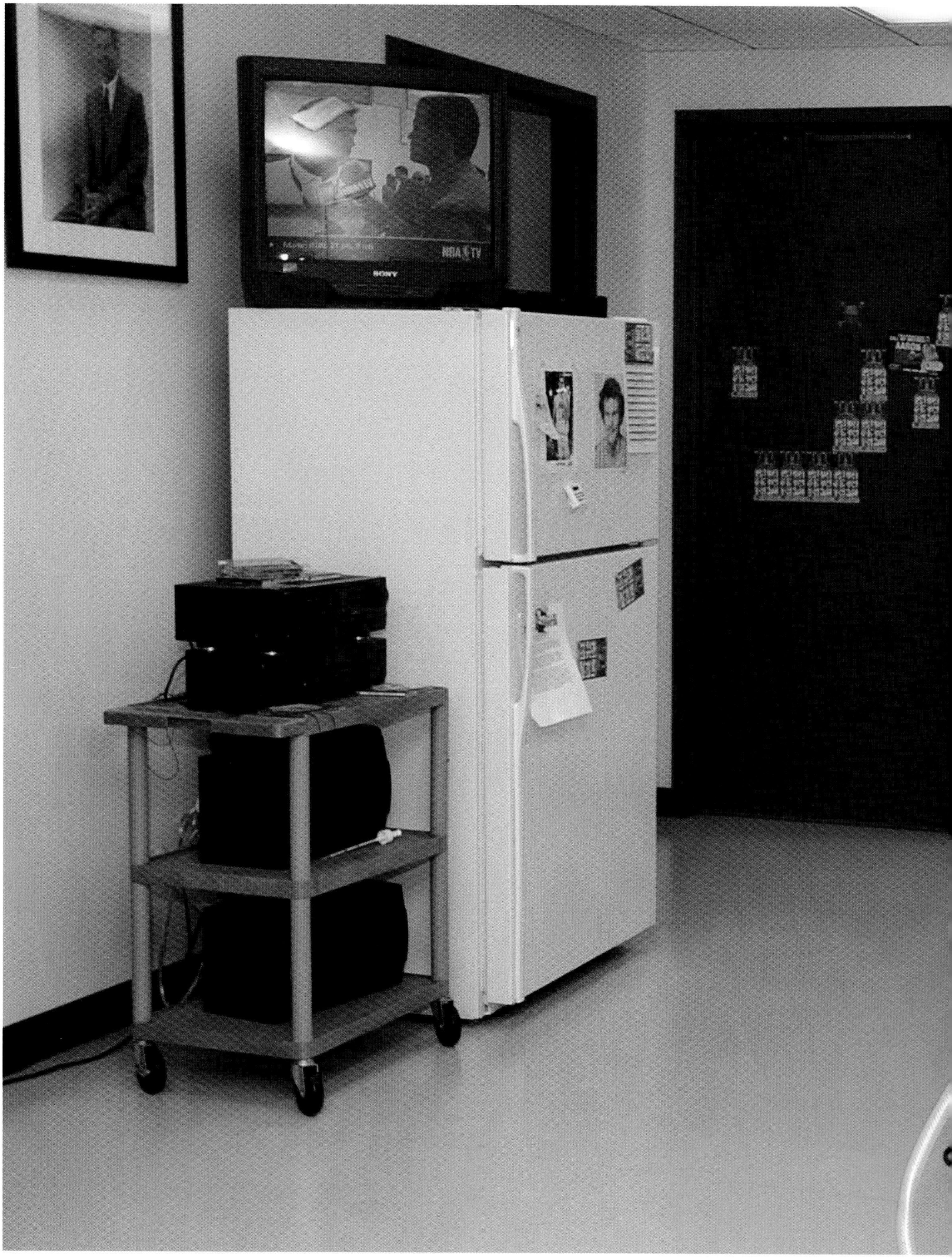
SONY
NBA TV
AARON

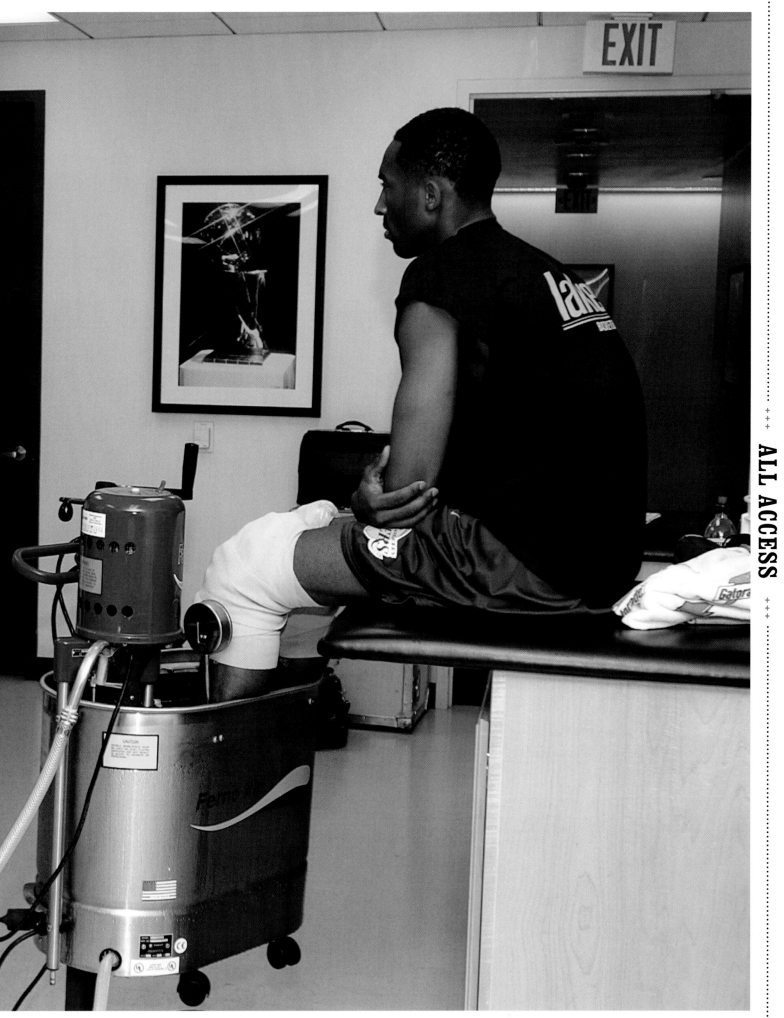

GAME
1234

"THE MADDER I GET,
THE MORE I DOMINATE."

+++ SHAQUILLE O'NEAL +++
40 POINTS, 12 REBOUNDS, 8 ASSISTS

# "We're not toying with them. We have the biggest, most dominant player on the planet. It would be tough for any team. Until they make more adjustments, we'll keep getting the ball to him."

+++ **Brian Shaw** +++

**I**t isn't a good idea to get Shaquille O'Neal mad. The last thing the New Jersey Nets wanted or needed, being down 0-1 in the NBA Finals against the heavily favored Los Angeles Lakers, was a grouchy 7-foot-1, 350-pound center ready to prove a point to the world on basketball's biggest stage. But that's exactly what happened when O'Neal heard comments from Sacramento Kings coach Rick Adelman in a television interview pertaining to his free-throw shooting. The inspiration turned into devastation for the Nets.

"The madder I get, the more I dominate," said O'Neal.

O'Neal's stat line for the game reflected the destruction that he inflicted on the Nets as he turned in perhaps his most dominant NBA Finals performance ever.

41 Minutes...40 Points...12 rebounds...8 assists...1 block...12-14 free throws.

From opening tipoff, O'Neal's focus never wavered, even as the Nets desperately tried to move him away from the basket. He was a one-man wrecking crew, putting on a dazzling display of moves that ranged from power dunks and jump hooks to perfectly delivered passes, including a beautiful no-look to a cutting Brian Shaw to the basket.

"This is not a fluke," said teammate Rick Fox. "This is what he does at this time of year. It's a big stage; the world is watching. He's been MVP of the last two [Finals], and he's going for three."

While the Lakers Superman was leaping off tall buildings, the Nets were grounded, struggling to score points. Jason Kidd was shut out in the first half, while his teammates Keith Van Horn and Kenyon Martin reflected the team's ineptness from the field, combining to hit 5 of 17 shots for 15 points for the game. Collectively, the Nets shot 34.9 percent.

"We're missing shots," said Nets coach Byron Scott. "That's the bottom line. We're getting the shots that we normally get in the regular season, shots that we've been getting throughout the playoffs and we're just missing them right now."

Despite the poor shooting, the Nets managed to close a 20-point gap down to six, with O'Neal on the bench at the end of third quarter, only to watch the Lakers run off a 12-0 spurt once he re-entered the game in the fourth.

Worse for the Nets was that O'Neal's big toe injury didn't appear to be the hindrance it was when the Lakers began their three-peat quest on April 21.

"He seemed to gather energy during the playoffs," said Lakers coach Phil Jackson. "That's been the remarkable part of it, that he's energized for the playoffs. This was his show." + + +

"What can I say?
Too much Shaquille O'Neal.
He's a monster."

+++ BYRON SCOTT +++

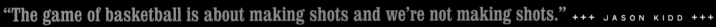

"The game of basketball is about making shots and we're not making shots." +++ JASON KIDD +++

## NEW JERSEY NETS

| PLAYER | POS | MIN | FGM-A | 3GM-A | FTM-A | OFF | DEF | TOT | AST | PF | ST | TO | BS | PTS |
|---|---|---|---|---|---|---|---|---|---|---|---|---|---|---|
| JASON KIDD | G | 39 | 6-17 | 3-8 | 2-3 | 4 | 5 | 9 | 7 | 3 | 2 | 5 | 1 | 17 |
| KERRY KITTLES | G | 29 | 9-19 | 3-9 | 2-4 | 1 | 2 | 3 | 3 | 4 | 2 | 1 | 1 | 23 |
| KENYON MARTIN | F | 35 | 2-8 | 0-1 | 2-4 | 2 | 3 | 5 | 2 | 5 | 3 | 4 | 0 | 6 |
| KEITH VAN HORN | F | 24 | 3-9 | 0-1 | 3-4 | 4 | 4 | 8 | 1 | 2 | 2 | 0 | 0 | 9 |
| TODD MACCULLOCH | C | 15 | 1-3 | 0-0 | 0-0 | 2 | 3 | 5 | 0 | 4 | 1 | 1 | 1 | 2 |
| Richard Jefferson | + | 32 | 3-6 | 0-0 | 4-8 | 2 | 3 | 5 | 3 | 2 | 0 | 1 | 0 | 10 |
| Jason Collins | + | 21 | 2-2 | 0-0 | 2-2 | 0 | 1 | 1 | 0 | 4 | 0 | 1 | 1 | 6 |
| Lucious Harris | + | 18 | 0-9 | 0-2 | 2-2 | 2 | 0 | 2 | 2 | 1 | 1 | 0 | 0 | 2 |
| Aaron Williams | + | 15 | 2-7 | 0-0 | 0-0 | 2 | 1 | 3 | 0 | 2 | 0 | 0 | 1 | 4 |
| Anthony Johnson | + | 10 | 2-5 | 0-0 | 0-0 | 1 | 1 | 2 | 0 | 0 | 0 | 0 | 0 | 4 |
| Donny Marshall | + | 1 | 0-1 | 0-1 | 0-0 | 0 | 0 | 0 | 0 | 0 | 0 | 0 | 0 | 0 |
| Brian Scalabrine | + | 1 | 0-0 | 0-0 | 0-0 | 0 | 0 | 0 | 0 | 0 | 0 | 0 | 0 | 0 |
| TOTAL | | 240 | 30-86 | 6-22 | 17-27 | 20 | 23 | 43 | 18 | 27 | 11 | 13 | 5 | 83 |
| | | | (34.9) | (27.3) | (63.0) | Team Rebs: 11 | | | | | | | | |

## LOS ANGELES LAKERS

| PLAYER | POS | MIN | FGM-A | 3GM-A | FTM-A | OFF | DEF | TOT | AST | PF | ST | TO | BS | PTS |
|---|---|---|---|---|---|---|---|---|---|---|---|---|---|---|
| KOBE BRYANT | G | 42 | 9-15 | 3-3 | 3-4 | 1 | 7 | 8 | 3 | 2 | 2 | 4 | 1 | 24 |
| DEREK FISHER | G | 29 | 4-9 | 2-3 | 2-4 | 2 | 3 | 5 | 3 | 5 | 0 | 2 | 0 | 12 |
| ROBERT HORRY | F | 43 | 4-9 | 1-3 | 0-0 | 4 | 6 | 10 | 4 | 2 | 3 | 2 | 3 | 9 |
| RICK FOX | F | 36 | 3-6 | 2-4 | 2-2 | 1 | 7 | 8 | 6 | 5 | 1 | 2 | 1 | 10 |
| SHAQUILLE O'NEAL | C | 41 | 14-23 | 0-0 | 12-14 | 3 | 9 | 12 | 8 | 2 | 0 | 4 | 1 | 40 |
| Brian Shaw | + | 22 | 2-6 | 1-2 | 0-0 | 0 | 2 | 2 | 2 | 2 | 0 | 1 | 1 | 5 |
| Devean George | + | 17 | 3-7 | 0-0 | 0-0 | 1 | 1 | 2 | 0 | 1 | 0 | 0 | 0 | 6 |
| Samaki Walker | + | 5 | 0-1 | 0-0 | 0-0 | 0 | 0 | 0 | 0 | 2 | 0 | 1 | 0 | 0 |
| Lindsey Hunter | + | 3 | 0-2 | 0-1 | 0-0 | 0 | 0 | 0 | 0 | 0 | 0 | 0 | 0 | 0 |
| Mark Madsen | + | 2 | 0-0 | 0-0 | 0-0 | 0 | 0 | 0 | 0 | 0 | 0 | 0 | 0 | 0 |
| Mitch Richmond | + | DNP | + | + | + | + | + | + | + | + | + | + | + | + |
| Stanislav Medvedenko | + | DNP | + | + | + | + | + | + | + | + | + | + | + | + |
| TOTAL | | 240 | 39-78 | 9-16 | 19-24 | 12 | 35 | 47 | 26 | 21 | 6 | 16 | 7 | 106 |
| | | | (50.0) | (56.3) | (79.2) | Team Rebs: 9 | | | | | | | | |

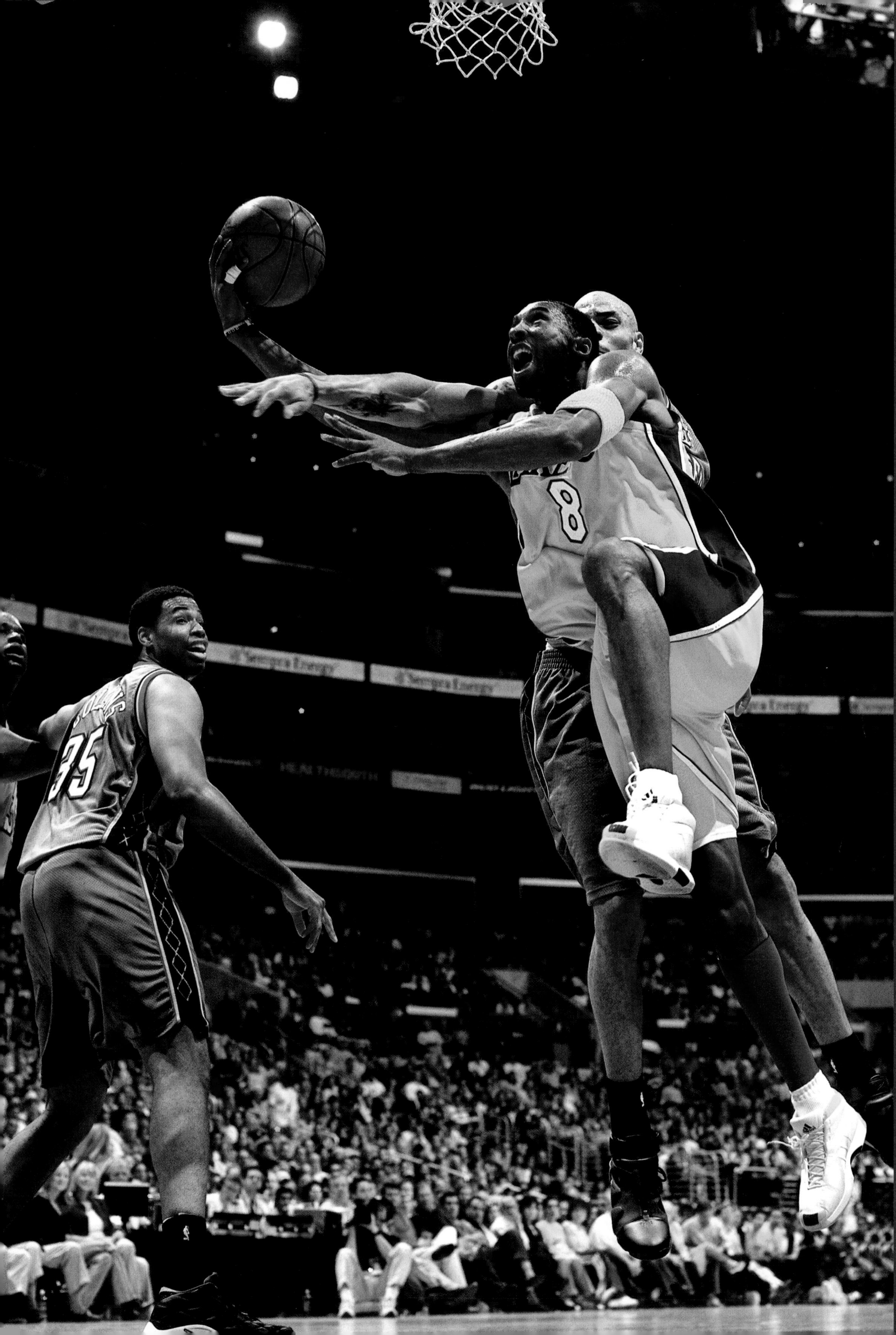
8
35

NBA FINALS 2002
LOVE IT LIVE

JACK NICHOLSON

DYAN CANNON

BILLY CRYSTAL & CHRIS ROCK

SALMA HAYEK

ELIZABETH SHUE

JAMES VAN DER BEEK

JENNA ELFMAN

BRAD PITT

MARK WAHLBERG

ELLEN DEGENERES

STEPHEN BALDWIN

JACK OSBOURNE

ANDY GARCIA

DREA de MATTEO

DANNY DEVITO & BOW WOW

JOHN LITHGOW

EDWARD NORTON

TOM ARNOLD

QUEEN LATIFAH

MICHELLE PFEIFFER & DAVID E. KELLEY

MIMI ROGERS

MATT DAMON, SALMA HAYEK & JEFFERY KATZENBERG

DAVID SCHWIMMER

PHIL & AMY MICKELSON

JULIE BOWEN & DAVID SPADE

NOAH WILEY

PETE SAMPRAS

PAULA ABDUL

TYSON BECKFORD

GREG KINNEAR

SPIKE LEE

SCOTT FOLEY

DON JOHNSON

JAY-Z

VANESSA WILLIAMS

DUSTIN HOFFMAN

NBA FINALS 2002
LOVE IT LIVE

JADA PINKETT SMITH

DONALD TRUMP & MELANIA KNAUSS

MICHAEL STRAHAN

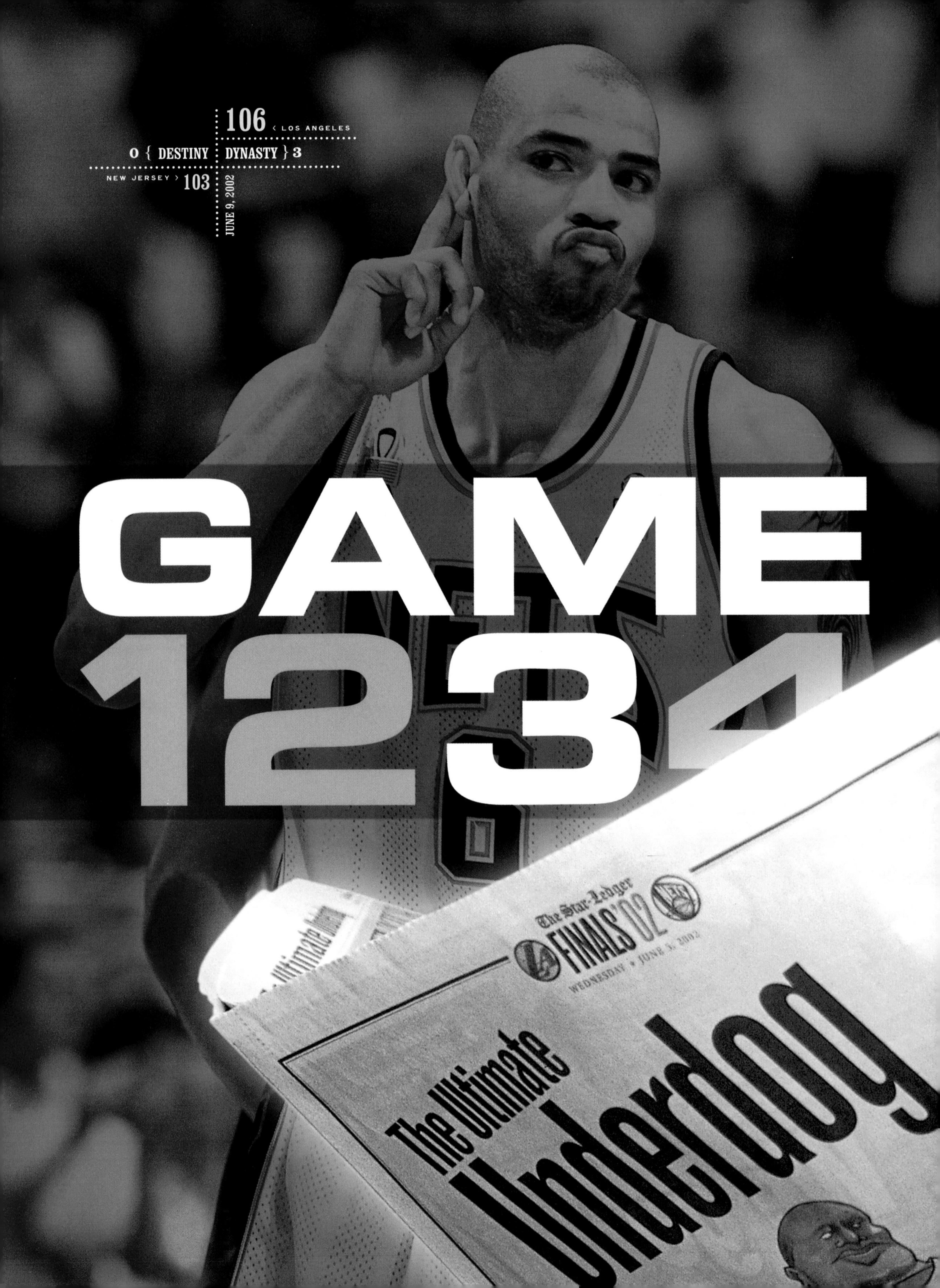

The Star-Ledger
FINALS '02
WEDNESDAY • JUNE 5, 2002
The Ultimate
Underdog

106 ‹ LOS ANGELES

0 { DESTINY | DYNASTY } 3

NEW JERSEY › 103

JUNE 9, 2002

# GAME
# 1234

"WE HAVEN'T GIVEN UP ALL YEAR. WE'LL CONTINUE TO FIGHT."

+ + + Keith Van Horn + + +

# "I'm here at home and, you know, we're here to do a job. Kobe won in his hometown last year, I have the opportunity to win in my hometown this year."

+++ **Shaquille O'Neal** +++

WHO WAS BORN IN NEWARK AND SPENT HIS PRE−TEEN YEARS IN NEW JERSEY,
BOUGHT 80 TICKETS FOR FAMILY AND FRIENDS FOR GAME 3.

The scene outside Continental Airlines Arena hours before tipoff gave no indication that the Nets were sinking in NBA Finals quicksand. Under a sun-drenched sky, long suffering fans were celebrating not only a beautiful Northern New Jersey summer-like day, but the fact that their beloved Nets were hosting an NBA Finals game for the very first time in franchise history. Music blared out of arena and car speakers as people of all ages wearing No. 5 jerseys danced at a feverish pace while Frisbees flew across the parking lot over a sea of sizzling, portable grills. Yes, Nets fans were *Loving It Live* in East Rutherford. Inside the arena, the Nets enjoyed a little home cooking of their own, as they had the two-time defending champs on the ropes, desperately hoping to get back into this series. Unfortunately for the Nets, the Lakers were the ones serving the dessert.

The Nets were clearly a different team at home, feeding off the emotion, energy and passion of the sold-out, delirious crowd. No player benefited more from this surge of support than Kenyon Martin, who struggled in the first two games, shooting a combined 9-30 (30.0 percent). This time, the 6-9 power forward was on his turf, running the floor with confidence, throwing down emotionally charged dunks on one end, playing spirited defense on the other.

The Lakers were prepared for such an onslaught not only from Martin but from the other players. They did their best to quiet the hostile crowd, owning a six-point halftime lead, thanks to Shaquille O'Neal's 21 points. The foundation appeared to be cracking for the Nets in the third as the Lakers' lead grew to double digits. The possibility of a three games to none lead looked more and more likely, except to one person— Jason Kidd. The All-Star guard single-handedly brought the Nets back from a 10-point deficit, scoring seven straight points and helping propel New Jersey to a 14-0 run to give them an 94-87 lead. The Nets, who lost the first two games by an average of 14 points, now found themselves in position to make it a 2-1 series, a thought that seemed highly unlikely less than 48 hours ago.

The stage was set for a climactic finish, as both teams felt the urgency to deliver the victory.

With the Nets now ahead by only one point, 96-95, Robert Horry—*surprise*—hit a clutch three-pointer to give L.A. a two-point lead with 3:03 left in regulation. After a Jason Kidd three-point miss, Kobe Bryant, who lives for the big moments, hit a difficult 22-foot jumper off the dribble with one second left on the shot clock for a 100-96 lead. A few possessions later, Bryant hit yet another difficult basket, this time a 10-footer in the lane over two defenders with 19.1 seconds left that gave L.A. a 104-100 lead.

"I wanted it," said Bryant who finished with a game high 36 points. "It's game time. I wasn't going to let them take it from me. We're battle-tested. That's what I kept telling the fellas in timeouts."

In the end, a spectacular game by Kidd, who had 30 points and 10 assists, wasn't enough to carry the Nets to the victory.

"We had a great opportunity," said Kidd. "It's not a blown opportunity. The better team won tonight." + + +

"He's a great player who played his heart out tonight."

+++ SHAQUILLE O'NEAL ON JASON KIDD'S 30 POINT, 10 ASSIST PERFORMANCE +++

"SHAQ IS GOLIATH. I WAS JUST PLAYING OFF HIM," SAID KOBE BRYANT, WHO SCORED 36 POINTS AND MADE TWO CLUTCH BASKETS DOWN THE STRETCH.

KENYON MARTIN BOUNCED BACK FROM SUBPAR
PERFORMANCES IN GAMES 1 AND 2 AND SPARKED NEW JERSEY'S
ATTACK WITH A 26-POINT EFFORT IN GAME 3.

"I THOUGHT KENYON WAS AWESOME."

+ + + Byron Scott + + +

SWAT! O'NEAL'S BLOCK OF JASON KIDD'S LEFT-HANDED LAYUP, WITH 48.3 SECONDS REMAINING IN REGULATION, WAS KEY IN SECURING THE LAKERS' 106–103 VICTORY.

## LOS ANGELES LAKERS

| PLAYER | POS | MIN | FGM-A | 3GM-A | FTM-A | OFF | DEF | TOT | AST | PF | ST | TO | BS | PTS |
|---|---|---|---|---|---|---|---|---|---|---|---|---|---|---|
| KOBE BRYANT | G | 46 | 14-23 | 1-3 | 7-10 | 1 | 5 | 6 | 4 | 3 | 1 | 6 | 2 | 36 |
| DEREK FISHER | G | 31 | 4-7 | 3-3 | 2-4 | 0 | 3 | 3 | 6 | 3 | 0 | 3 | 0 | 13 |
| RICK FOX | F | 37 | 2-6 | 1-3 | 2-2 | 0 | 4 | 4 | 2 | 2 | 1 | 3 | 1 | 7 |
| ROBERT HORRY | F | 31 | 2-4 | 2-3 | 0-0 | 0 | 7 | 7 | 3 | 5 | 3 | 3 | 1 | 6 |
| SHAQUILLE O'NEAL | C | 42 | 12-19 | 0-0 | 11-17 | 5 | 6 | 11 | 2 | 1 | 0 | 2 | 4 | 35 |
| Devean George | + | 24 | 2-4 | 0-0 | 2-2 | 1 | 7 | 8 | 0 | 3 | 1 | 1 | 2 | 6 |
| Brian Shaw | + | 17 | 1-4 | 1-4 | 0-0 | 0 | 1 | 1 | 0 | 0 | 1 | 1 | 0 | 3 |
| Samaki Walker | + | 6 | 0-1 | 0-0 | 0-0 | 0 | 0 | 0 | 0 | 1 | 0 | 0 | 0 | 0 |
| Stanislav Medvedenko | + | 4 | 0-0 | 0-0 | 0-0 | 0 | 0 | 0 | 0 | 2 | 0 | 0 | 0 | 0 |
| Lindsey Hunter | + | 2 | 0-0 | 0-0 | 0-0 | 0 | 0 | 0 | 0 | 2 | 0 | 0 | 0 | 0 |
| Mark Madsen | + | DNP | + | + | + | + | + | + | + | + | + | + | + | + |
| Mitch Richmond | + | DNP | + | + | + | + | + | + | + | + | + | + | + | + |
| TOTAL | | 240 | 37-68 | 8-16 | 24-35 | 7 | 33 | 40 | 17 | 22 | 7 | 19 | 10 | 106 |
| | | | (54.4) | (50.0) | (68.6) | Team Rebs: 11 | | | | | | | | |

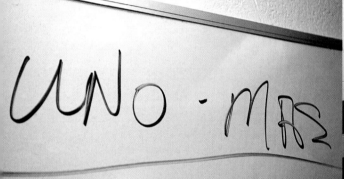

## NEW JERSEY NETS

| PLAYER | POS | MIN | FGM-A | 3GM-A | FTM-A | OFF | DEF | TOT | AST | PF | ST | TO | BS | PTS |
|---|---|---|---|---|---|---|---|---|---|---|---|---|---|---|
| JASON KIDD | G | 43 | 13-23 | 1-5 | 3-5 | 1 | 4 | 5 | 10 | 3 | 3 | 2 | 1 | 30 |
| KERRY KITTLES | G | 29 | 3-6 | 0-2 | 1-2 | 1 | 2 | 3 | 3 | 1 | 3 | 0 | 0 | 7 |
| KENYON MARTIN | F | 43 | 11-17 | 0-1 | 4-6 | 1 | 3 | 4 | 4 | 3 | 2 | 5 | 2 | 26 |
| KEITH VAN HORN | F | 31 | 6-14 | 2-4 | 0-0 | 0 | 5 | 5 | 3 | 5 | 0 | 0 | 1 | 14 |
| TODD MACCULLOCH | C | 14 | 4-8 | 0-0 | 2-2 | 0 | 1 | 1 | 0 | 3 | 0 | 2 | 1 | 10 |
| Jason Collins | + | 27 | 0-4 | 0-0 | 2-2 | 2 | 1 | 3 | 0 | 4 | 0 | 2 | 0 | 2 |
| Richard Jefferson | + | 22 | 4-5 | 0-0 | 0-0 | 0 | 3 | 3 | 0 | 1 | 2 | 2 | 0 | 8 |
| Lucious Harris | + | 19 | 1-5 | 0-0 | 0-0 | 0 | 3 | 3 | 2 | 1 | 3 | 0 | 0 | 2 |
| Aaron Williams | + | 7 | 1-1 | 0-0 | 2-2 | 0 | 0 | 0 | 0 | 6 | 0 | 0 | 0 | 4 |
| Anthony Johnson | + | 5 | 0-0 | 0-0 | 0-0 | 0 | 0 | 0 | 0 | 0 | 0 | 0 | 0 | 0 |
| Donny Marshall | + | DNP | + | + | + | + | + | + | + | + | + | + | + | + |
| Brian Scalabrine | + | DNP | + | + | + | + | + | + | + | + | + | + | + | + |
| TOTAL | | 240 | 43-83 | 3-12 | 14-19 | 5 | 22 | 27 | 22 | 27 | 13 | 13 | 5 | 103 |
| | | | (51.8) | (25.0) | (73.7) | Team Rebs: 9 | | | | | | | | |

"Kobe made some big shots down the stretch. I tried to do the same thing. We just came up short." +++ JASON KIDD +++

JASON KIDD AND KOBE BRYANT STARRED IN PRODUCING
A DRAMATIC GAME 3 FINISH.

113 ‹ LOS ANGELES
0 { DESTINY : DYNASTY } 4
NEW JERSEY › 107

JUNE 12, 2002

# GAME
# 1234

"WE'RE A GREAT TEAM AND EVERYBODY STUCK TO THEIR ROLE, EVERYBODY
STUCK TO THE SCRIPT, EVERYBODY BELIEVED."

+++ SHAQUILLE O'NEAL +++

# "Three in a row is unbelievable. One was great, then we got two, three we sweep. Just unbelievable!"

+++ **Rick Fox** +++

he journey to the elite class of NBA champions began for Shaquille O'Neal approximately 21 hours before tip off. The Newark, N.J., native paid a special visit to his roots, the place where it all began. A place where his championship hopes, dreams and visions first took shape.

"I went to Weequahic Park where I first started...last night about 12," said O'Neal of the place often referred to as The Hole. "As a youngster, I used to just play with the raggedy basketball my father got me. I used to dream about certain things. I just stuck with it. All my dreams have come true."

Some 24 hours later, they certainly did. Shaq and the Lakers had completed the sweep of the New Jersey Nets with a 113-107 victory that not only cemented his status as one of the all-time great centers in the history of the game but also

established the Lakers as one of the best teams of the modern era.

"We're a great team and everybody stuck to their role, everybody stuck to the script, everybody believed," said O'Neal, who dedicated the championship to his grandmother who passed away earlier in the season. "Nobody ever got down, even, you know, when times were so-called hard."

O'Neal's 34 points and 10 rebounds helped secure his third consecutive NBA Finals MVP award, an honor shared only by Michael Jordan of the Chicago Bulls. O'Neal also set a Finals record for most points scored in a four-game series, with 145, besting the old mark of 131 established by Hakeem Olajuwon of the Houston Rockets. Ironically, Olajuwon performed this feat against O'Neal and the Orlando Magic in the 1995 Finals.

The Nets didn't go down without a fight, as they desperately tried to keep the series alive.

Second-year forward Kenyon Martin carried the team with a 35-point, 11-rebound performance, which included 17 points in the first quarter. Martin's teammate, Jason Kidd, added 13 points and 12 assists, but it wasn't enough to ensure this team of Destiny an opportunity to play another day.

"It hurts," said Kidd of the sweep. "There's a little sting because we couldn't win. You know, we wanted to win one game. We felt if we could win one game, that would give us some confidence."

Now the talk officially begins: Where do these three-time NBA champion Lakers reside in the pantheon of all-time great NBA dynasties?

"I don't know about ranking among the great teams ever," said a jovial Bryant after the game. "We really have to stand the test of time. I think it's a little too early right now." + + +

## LOS ANGELES LAKERS

| PLAYER | POS | MIN | FGM-A | 3GM-A | FTM-A | OFF | DEF | TOT | AST | PF | ST | TO | BS | PTS |
|---|---|---|---|---|---|---|---|---|---|---|---|---|---|---|
| KOBE BRYANT | G | 44 | 7-16 | 2-3 | 9-11 | 0 | 6 | 6 | 8 | 4 | 2 | 1 | 0 | 25 |
| DEREK FISHER | G | 36 | 5-10 | 2-4 | 1-2 | 0 | 5 | 5 | 4 | 1 | 0 | 0 | 0 | 13 |
| ROBERT HORRY | F | 44 | 3-5 | 2-3 | 4-4 | 1 | 3 | 4 | 6 | 4 | 2 | 1 | 1 | 12 |
| RICK FOX | F | 32 | 2-3 | 2-3 | 2-2 | 0 | 5 | 5 | 3 | 2 | 2 | 4 | 0 | 8 |
| SHAQUILLE O'NEAL | C | 43 | 12-20 | 0-0 | 10-16 | 3 | 7 | 10 | 4 | 2 | 1 | 3 | 2 | 34 |
| Devean George | + | 20 | 4-7 | 3-4 | 0-0 | 2 | 4 | 6 | 0 | 1 | 0 | 0 | 0 | 11 |
| Brian Shaw | + | 15 | 3-9 | 0-2 | 0-0 | 1 | 1 | 2 | 3 | 0 | 0 | 0 | 0 | 6 |
| Samaki Walker | + | 5 | 0-0 | 0-0 | 2-2 | 0 | 1 | 1 | 0 | 1 | 0 | 0 | 0 | 2 |
| Mitch Richmond | + | 1 | 1-1 | 0-0 | 0-0 | 0 | 0 | 0 | 0 | 0 | 0 | 0 | 0 | 2 |
| Mark Madsen | + | DNP | + | + | + | + | + | + | + | + | + | + | + | + |
| Lindsey Hunter | + | DNP | + | + | + | + | + | + | + | + | + | + | + | + |
| Stanislav Medvedenko | + | DNP | + | + | + | + | + | + | + | + | + | + | + | + |
| TOTAL | | 240 | 37-71 | 11-19 | 28-37 | 7 | 32 | 39 | 28 | 15 | 7 | 9 | 3 | 113 |
| | | | (52.1) | (57.9) | (75.7) | Team Rebs: 5 | | | | | | | | |

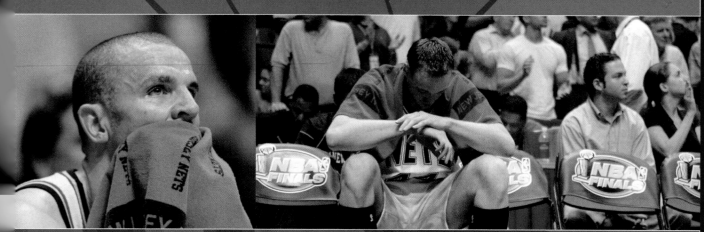

## NEW JERSEY NETS

| PLAYER | POS | MIN | FGM-A | 3GM-A | FTM-A | OFF | DEF | TOT | AST | PF | ST | TO | BS | PTS |
|---|---|---|---|---|---|---|---|---|---|---|---|---|---|---|
| JASON KIDD | G | 43 | 5-14 | 1-4 | 2-2 | 1 | 4 | 5 | 12 | 1 | 1 | 4 | 1 | 13 |
| KERRY KITTLES | G | 23 | 4-10 | 1-3 | 2-2 | 2 | 0 | 2 | 3 | 1 | 1 | 1 | 0 | 11 |
| KENYON MARTIN | F | 43 | 15-28 | 0-0 | 5-7 | 2 | 9 | 11 | 2 | 4 | 1 | 2 | 1 | 35 |
| KEITH VAN HORN | F | 31 | 3-7 | 1-1 | 0-0 | 1 | 3 | 4 | 4 | 2 | 0 | 1 | 0 | 7 |
| TODD MACCULLOCH | C | 20 | 4-8 | 0-0 | 0-0 | 4 | 2 | 6 | 2 | 4 | 0 | 0 | 1 | 8 |
| Lucious Harris | + | 29 | 9-13 | 1-1 | 3-4 | 2 | 1 | 3 | 2 | 1 | 0 | 0 | 0 | 22 |
| Richard Jefferson | + | 21 | 2-6 | 0-0 | 1-1 | 0 | 4 | 4 | 1 | 1 | 1 | 0 | 0 | 5 |
| Jason Collins | + | 19 | 2-3 | 0-0 | 0-0 | 1 | 3 | 4 | 0 | 6 | 1 | 0 | 1 | 4 |
| Aaron Williams | + | 9 | 1-3 | 0-0 | 0-0 | 1 | 1 | 2 | 0 | 2 | 0 | 0 | 0 | 2 |
| Donny Marshall | + | 1 | 0-0 | 0-0 | 0-0 | 0 | 0 | 0 | 0 | 0 | 0 | 0 | 0 | 0 |
| Anthony Johnson | + | 1 | 0-0 | 0-0 | 0-0 | 0 | 0 | 0 | 1 | 0 | 0 | 0 | 0 | 0 |
| Brian Scalabrine | + | DNP | + | + | + | + | + | + | + | + | + | + | + | + |
| TOTAL | | 240 | 45-92 | 4-9 | 13-16 | 14 | 27 | 41 | 27 | 22 | 5 | 8 | 4 | 107 |
| | | | (48.9) | (44.4) | (81.3) | Team Rebs: 8 | | | | | | | | |

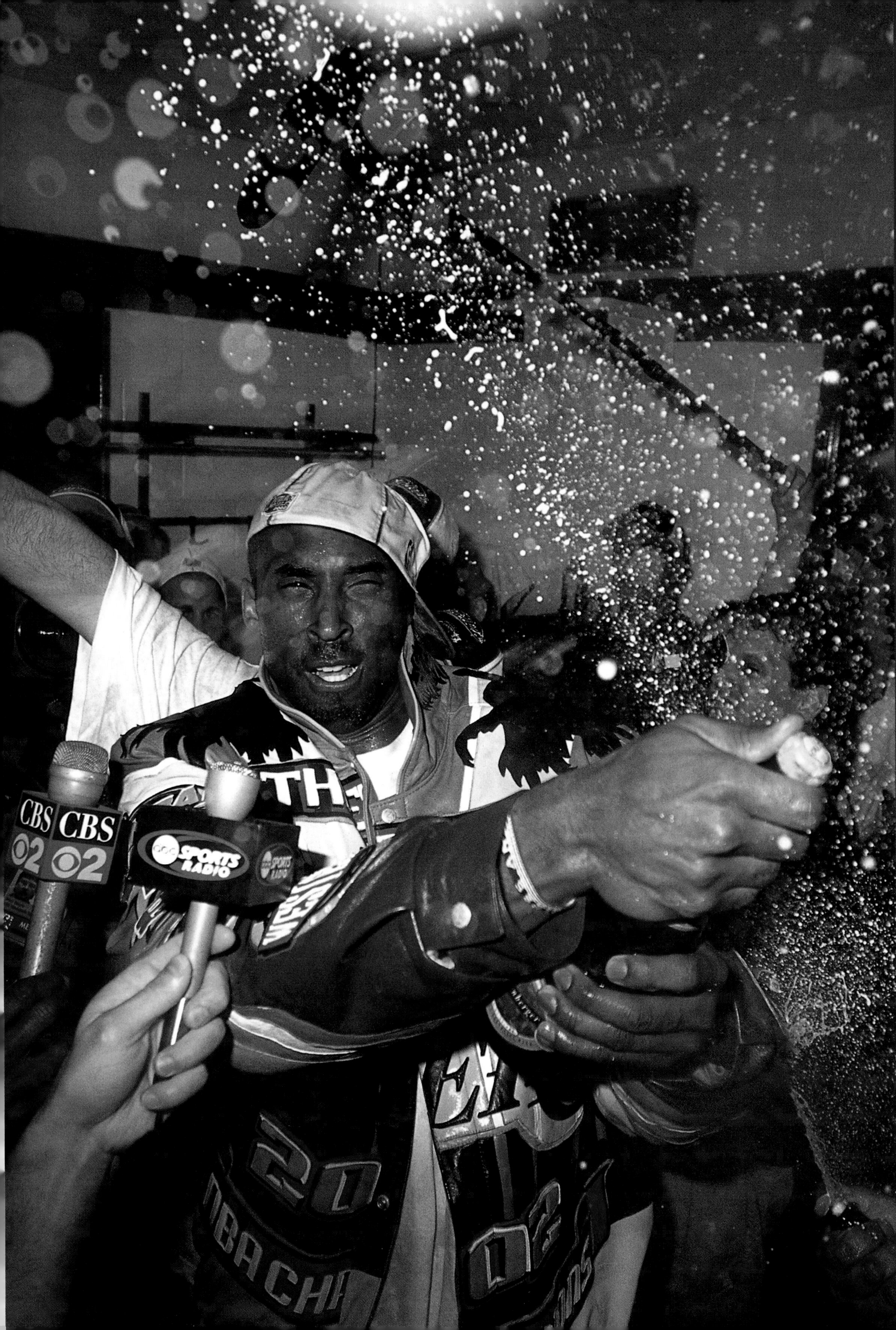
CBS
CBS
SPORTS RADIO